Practical LEGO Technics

Bring Your LEGO Creations to Life

Mark Rollins

Apress®

Practical LEGO Technics: Bring Your LEGO Creations to Life

ISBN-13 (pbk): 978-1-4302-4611-4

ISBN-13 (electronic): 978-1-4302-4612-1

President and Publisher: Paul Manning
Lead Editor: Michelle Lowman
Developmental Editors: James Markham
Technical Reviewer: Jon Lazar
Editorial Board: Steve Anglin, Ewan Buckingham, Gary Cornell, Louise Corrigan, Morgan Ertel, Jonathan Gennick, Jonathan Hassell, Robert Hutchinson, Michelle Lowman, James Markham, Matthew Moodie, Jeff Olson, Jeffrey Pepper, Douglas Pundick, Ben Renow-Clarke, Dominic Shakeshaft, Gwenan Spearing, Matt Wade, Tom Welsh
Coordinating Editor: Katie Sullivan
Copy Editor: Mary Behr
Compositor: Bytheway Publishing Services
Indexer: SPi Global
Artist: SPi Global
Cover Designer: Anna Ishchenko

Distributed to the book trade worldwide by Springer Science+Business Media New York, 233 Spring Street, 6th Floor, New York, NY 10013. Phone 1-800-SPRINGER, fax (201) 348-4505, e-mail orders-ny@springer-sbm.com, or visit www.springeronline.com.

For information on translations, please e-mail rights@apress.com, or visit www.apress.com.

Apress and friends of ED books may be purchased in bulk for academic, corporate, or promotional use. eBook versions and licenses are also available for most titles. For more information, reference our Special Bulk Sales–eBook Licensing web page at www.apress.com/bulk-sales.

Any source code or other supplementary materials referenced by the author in this text is available to readers at www.apress.com. For detailed information about how to locate your book's source code, go to www.apress.com/source-code.

Dedicated to all LEGO builders of all ages.

—Mark Rollins

Contents at a Glance

Contents

About the Author

Mark Rollins was born in Seattle in 1971, and attended Washington State University in Pullman, Washington. After four years, he graduated in 1994 with a degree in English. After college, he began to write skits for college-age groups. After four years working for Wal-Mart and another five years working for Schweitzer Engineering Laboratories (SEL), Mark decided to pursue a full-time career in writing, beginning in 2005.

Since then, he has written for many tech and gadget blogs including www.screenhead.com, www.image-acquire.com, www.cybertheater.com, www.mobilewhack.com, carbuyersnotebook.com, www.gearlive.com, www.zmogo.com, gadgetell.com, www.gadgets-weblog.com, www.androidedge.com, and www.coolest-gadgets.com. He has also written for video game blogs such as www.gamertell.com and www.digitalbattle.com.

In 2009, Mark decided to create his own tech and gadget blog known as www.TheGeekChurch.com. The purpose of the blog was to report on the latest in technology, as well as to inform the church-going crowd (who are often not very technically adept) on the benefits of using more technology in the ministry. Since 2012, Mark has completed devoted his time to this blog and considers it his ministry and mission.

Mark currently resides in Pullman, Washington with his wife and three children.

About the Technical Reviewer

 **Jon Lazar** is a freelance developer and social media consultant with 10+ years of experience in the technology field. He started his career at AT&T and has since helped a number of startups in the NYC area in building their digital presences and digital infrastructures. In his free time, he is an accomplished builder of LEGO sculptures. He regularly writes about LEGO, social media, technology, and other related topics on www.justjon.net.

Acknowledgments

I remember when I first discovered LEGO again. It was in the summer of 1984, I was fresh out of sixth grade, and I was visiting my friend's house. My friend showed me this Lego spaceship he had made that was 4.5 feet long, resting on a pool table. I thought it was one of the coolest things that I had ever seen; it was quite detailed. At that time, it had been a year or so since I had played with my LEGO bricks. I had a handful of sets that were just kept in a boxes and I thought that I had outgrown them. After visiting my friend's place, I started building again.

I kept building with LEGO, and I am now 40 years old. Now I have accrued many sets and have filled two large boxes with pieces. I have kids of my own, but if I wasn't so busy writing and being a father, I would create worlds for LEGO minifigs and build just about every machine that I could with these bricks.

This book is for any LEGO builder that dares to dream and then build what they can imagine.

I would also like to dedicate this book to my wife, who showed me how to do a "photobox" that helped me to photograph my LEGO creations.

Also helpful were Katie Sullivan and James Markham, the editorial team from Apress who made this project much easier.

—Mark Rollins

Introduction

During the 1980s, the LEGO company used the phrase "Toys to Grow Up With" as their slogan. While many play with these "toys" at a young age, most stop playing with LEGO as they reach adolescence. I stopped playing when I was 12, simply because I thought this is what a person of my age was "supposed" to do. Even though I had "quit" LEGO building, I never got rid of my old LEGO sets. Eventually, I remembered the joy that building with LEGO had brought me and went back to building.

Like it or not, LEGO is one of the easiest ways that a child or adult can create. A LEGO user is not required to draw or sculpt in order to make masterpieces, and the only tools required are their bare hands with very standardized pieces. The LEGO medium snaps together quite easily and can come apart just as easily. Originally, LEGO pieces were square and rectangular, but the company has made their bricks much more advanced, and an experienced LEGO builder can create something as curvaceous as the F-14 jet in Figure A-1.

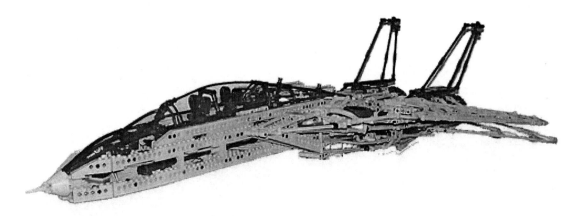

Figure A-1. According to the Raw art Weblog site (www.rawartint.com), this F-14 jet helped LEGO designer Jeroen Ottens land a job as a LEGO Technic designer. I too would have welcomed him aboard.

This book is for everyone like me who will never stop playing with LEGO, even though some might think that we are not "acting our age." My response to that crowd is, "it isn't playing, it is building" and "if it is child's play, then let's see you build that F-14." Man, would I love to give these naysayers the correct amount of bricks and watch them attempt to create some of the LEGO wonders that can be seen at various

LEGO theme parks in Florida and California. I'll bet many of them couldn't build a complex structure like the Sydney Opera House, even with a proper set of instructions.

The LEGO Technic or "Expert Builder" Collection

In Christmas of 1982, I received my first LEGO Technic set, 948 (the Go-Kart). I was about 10 at the time, and the suggested age for these LEGO sets was 9 and up. Before that, I was playing with a few modeling kits, including some of the first Space LEGO sets. I considered this Expert Builder set to be a challenge, and it was.

The Technic kits were a quantum leap from what I had been playing with before. Even though they used a lot of the usual bricks that I was used to, many of the bricks had holes in the sides. Other pieces, such as the axles, connector pins, and gears, looked strange to me. Considering that the basic LEGO construction is from the bottom up, the LEGO Technic allows the user to build out from the sides, which allows for a lot of "out-of-the-box" thinking.

LEGO Technic is able to be an educational toy while still remaining fun at the same time. And when I say "fun," I am not talking about mindless amusement like watching bad television, but the type of fun that involves the brain, like Sudoku or crossword puzzles. LEGO actually makes children think more, and the Technic sets teach a lot about basic machinery. Children are often quite curious about how things like automobiles and other technological wonders work, but as adults, we don't care about *how* machines work but rather *that* our machines work. With LEGO Technic, my technological curiosity was well-sated.

With LEGO Technic, I learned that steering is not just turning the wheel and the tires just move. I saw that a steering mechanism was no longer magic, but the simple application of rack and pinion technology. I even found that the steering wheel in my LEGO Go-Kart was not too different from what most cars actually use to steer.

Over the years, these expert sets became increasingly more complex. LEGO Technic is not to be confused with the LEGO Mindstorms series, although there are a lot of similarities. Apress has published many books about that particular series if you are interested in building more programmable LEGO Creations, such as:

- *Winning Design! LEGO MINDSTORMS NXT Design Patterns for Fun and Competition* by James Jeffrey Trobaugh (Apress, 2010).

- *LEGO Spybotics Secret Agent Training Manual* by Ralph Hempel (Apress, 2002).

- *LEGO MINDSTORMS NXT: Mars Base Command* by James Floyd Kelly (Apress, 2006).

- *LEGO MINDSTORMS NXT-G Programming Guide* (First and Second Editions) by James Floyd Kelly (Apress, 2007 and 2011).

- *LEGO MINDSTORMS NXT 2.0 The King's Treasure* by James Floyd Kelly (Apress, 2009).

- *LEGO MINDSTORMS NXT The Mayan Adventure* by James Floyd Kelly (Apress, 2006).

- *Extreme NXT: Extending the LEGO MINDSTORMS NXT to the Next Level* (First and Second Editions) by Michael Gasperi and Philippe E. Hurbain (Apress, 2007 and 2009).

- *Extreme MINDSTORMS An Advanced Guide to LEGO MINDSTORMS* by Michael Gasperi, Ralph Hempel, Luis Villa, and Dave Baum (Apress, 2000).

- *Creating Cool MINDSTORMS NXT Robots* by Daniele Benedettelli (Apress, 2008).

- *Dave Baum's Definitive Guide to LEGO MINDSTORMS*, Second Edition by Dave Baum (Apress, 2002).

- *Competitive MINDSTORMS, A Complete Guide to Robotic Sumo Using LEGO MINDSTORMS* by David J. Perdue (Apress, 2004).

How To Use This Book

I have seen a lot of interesting books about LEGO, and many of these "idea books" show a model so you can imitate it yourself, piece by piece. There is nothing wrong with copying, as learning by repetition and the imitation of what has come before is the only way we can advance to build more original and improved models. After all, you cannot solve complex differential equations unless you have learned 2 + 2. However, true mathematics involves discovery of new problems, solutions, and equations—and textbook problems must be left behind for that to happen.

What I don't want to do is show how to create a Corvette, and then have you, the reader, just follow the numbered steps to create one of your own at home. Instead, I want to show you how to make a successful LEGO frame for a vehicle, how to motorize and take remote control of it with Power Functions, and how add other features onto your LEGO creation to make it as lifelike as possible (in a scale model a fraction of its size).

What you will see in this book are designs to help you create LEGO Technic masterpieces, and I will show you basic ways to do basic functions on a LEGO Technic creation. What you will see in this book are some models that were created with the help several programs, which include LEGO Digital Designer and LDraw. This is not meant to be a book with just fully completed models. I could have done so by creating a wordless book where all you do is just work LEGO steps one through whatever. To heck with that! The real challenge (and fun) of LEGO is to create something very new, something that no one has built before. I guarantee that you will feel quite a surge as you apply some new method of LEGO technology to your own creation. To me, nothing beats the rush of creating something new, and I hope to share that with you.

In other words, think of this book as an abridged LEGO cookbook. I will show you how to make complex ingredients, and you will need to decide how best to combine these complex ingredients together to make some terrific LEGO Technic recipes.

How This Book Is Ordered

I organized the chapters in a way that they build upon each other, and if you want to skip ahead to chapters because you feel that you have already mastered the ones that came before it, please don't feel that I would be somehow offended. I fully realize that most books don't recommend skipping chapters, but this book permits you to do whatever is valuable to you as far as LEGO Technic is concerned.

- **Chapter 1: Getting Started with LEGO Technic.** This is essentially a chapter for those who have never seen LEGO Technic before. I introduce readers to the Technic bricks and how they differ from traditional LEGO bricks. I also showcase various software programs so that you can design LEGO models on your computer before building them with real LEGO bricks, and where to order Technic bricks in case you need a fresh supply.

- **Chapter 2: Creating a Motorized LEGO Technic Vehicle.** In this chapter, I introduce how the LEGO Power Functions pieces can be used to create a basic model of a wheeled vehicle. I show how to create a frame for a LEGO automobile and how Power Functions can make it go.

- **Chapter 3: Steering and Controlling Your LEGO Technic Creation.** This chapter is about creating a steering mechanism on your Technic vehicle, so you can not only make it go but give it direction as well.

- **Chapter 4: Light it up with LEGO lights!** This chapter discusses how to use the light pieces to create the wonder of light on your LEGO vehicles and how to really make them illuminated.

- **Chapter 5: Creating an All-Terrain LEGO Technic Vehicle.** For a lot of LEGO wheeled models, it is about taking a wheeled vehicle over all terrains. For this, you will need steering pieces or even special spring loaded pieces that will be helpful for taking your LEGO creation over all kinds of LEGO bricks and more. This chapter also shows how to create a LEGO Technic vehicle that has four-wheel drive.

- **Chapter 6: Technic Construction Vehicles and Equipment.** In this chapter, I cover how to assemble features on a LEGO model that you would be used at a construction site. I'm talking about swivels, bulldozer scoops, cranes, and dump truck mechanisms.

- **Chapter 7: LEGO Technic Aviation: Airplanes and Helicopters.** This chapter is about creating airplanes with working propellers, building wings with flaps that can be adjusted by controls on the plane itself, and constructing stable landing gear and one that can retract. Sadly, I can't figure out how to make the planes fly, but perhaps in the future all LEGO models will.

■ ■ ■

CHAPTER 1

Getting Started with LEGO Technic

LEGO is no longer just for children, and the Technic series encourages both children and adults to build complex vehicles and machines from these simple bricks. The purpose of this book is to show you how to create interesting LEGO Technic creations, but I fully encourage your own creativity and improvisation.

I figure that there are two types of people reading this book. There are those folks who have been playing with LEGO for as long as they can remember (perhaps in their Duplo or Quattro days) and are quite familiar with traditional LEGO pieces. The second type is just starting with LEGO Technic. Ideally, I hope that you are an adult trying to teach a child or teenager how machines work via the power of LEGO.

If you are of the second type, you are probably wondering where to begin. You also probably can't wait to get started building some of the models you saw when you flipped through the printed book or previewed the e-book. It's fully possible to construct these models in a digital program, and there are a few programs devoted to LEGO building that I will detail later. However, if you are like me, then you want to build these LEGO models in real life—and even play with them. Yeah, you know what I'm talking about.

My first bit of advice is to make certain that you have all the pieces that you need before you begin building. This is why all the steps of my LEGO models include a list (with pictures) of the necessary parts. There is even a list of all the parts for each model in the Appendix. LEGO Technic bricks differ from that of traditional sets, and if you are looking for certain pieces, I recommend LEGO Pick a Brick or other online LEGO catalogs like BrickLink.com for getting the components you need. I will discuss those online catalogs later, but right now I want to discuss the different types of LEGO Technic pieces including bricks, beams, levers, gears, racks, axles, bushes, connector pegs, cross blocks, angle elements, steering parts, and more.

A Guide to Technic LEGO Pieces

Let's start with a basic introduction to Technic LEGO pieces.

Technic Bricks

Technic Bricks are just like traditional LEGO bricks but with holes on the sides for axles and connector pegs (see Figure 1-1). Bricks, like most LEGO pieces, are measured by the amount of studs (the round bumpy parts atop a normal LEGO brick) on them, and this measurement is often abbreviated to M. Generally, the number of side holes is always one less than the studs, but there are some, like the 1 x 1 x 1 and 2 x 1 x 1, with the same amount of side holes as studs. There are some interesting methods to these pieces; for instance, the 2 x 1 x 1 has an axle or a cross-shaped hole. Note the variations with the Technic fork and wing sections. There are even more interesting forms with the Angular Brick 5 x 5, 4 x 4, 4 x 6, and 6 x 8 pieces.

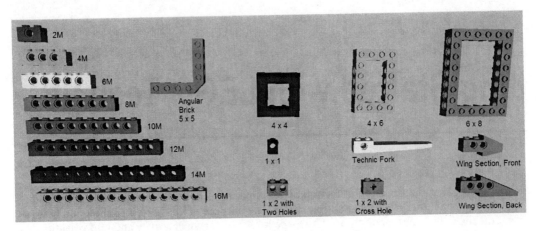

Figure 1-1. Some traditional LEGO Technic bricks

These bricks are not included in the recent Technic sets since the switch to more "studless" forms, but they were the groundbreaking bricks of the first generation of Technic, the Expert Builders. This book is full of LEGO Technic models, but very few will be using this type of LEGO Technic pieces. The majority of models in this book will be made with studless beams.

Beams

Circa 2000, Technic became less about actual bricks with studs and more about beams. Many of the Technic sets do not have any traditional studded bricks. Some people have stated that the studless construction makes it harder to build a LEGO Technic model, and I will have to say that I agree with them.

The issue with the studless beams and other parts is that you must have a good idea of the shape of your finished product before you begin to build. Fortunately, there is always room for improving your model, and in some cases studless bricks can be replaced more easily than traditional top-down traditional LEGO bricks. Each beam is about as thick as a 1 x 1 brick, and they are measured just like their studded counterparts: based on the number of studs they take up. The difference between studded bricks and studless beams is that the measurement of a beam is always equal to the number of holes on it. The straight beams in Figure 1-2 are designated with a number; this is so you can quickly determine the beam that you need without doing too much hole counting. While LEGO Technic studded bricks are usually even-numbered, LEGO beams are usually odd-numbered, with the exception of the 2M.

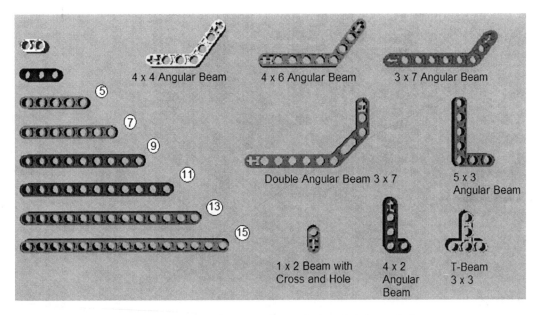

Figure 1-2. LEGO Technic beams including straight, angled, and right angled

You will notice that the beams come in a variety of angles. The 4 x 4 Angular Beam, 4 x 6 Angular Beam, and 3 x 7 Angular Beam are at 53.1 degrees, and the Double Angular Beam 3 x 7 offers two angles. The 90 degree angle pieces include the 3 x 5, 4 x 2, and the 3 x 3 T-Beam.

Another thing that you will notice about some of the angular pieces is that they end with cross holes. These are made to hold axles, and any axle inserted in these cross holes is well anchored. The 1 x 2 beam has a cross and hole, making it useful in all manner of ways.

Levers

This is a very broad category of Technic pieces, and the first thing you should know about them is that a lever is half has thick as a beam. In other words, you must stack two levers together to form something the width of a beam.

The levers in sizes 4M and below have cross-shaped openings that accommodate an axle (also known as a cross hole) at their ends, while the 5M half beams are made for loosely accepting connector pins and axles. Levers are often used for joining two beams together. Note the other odd shapes like the Comb Wheel, 3 x 120, and the Triangle. They also come in a simple 3 x 3 90 degree formation as well as some fancy half beam curves that also do a 90 degree angle with three different measurements (see Figure 1-3). Note the variation of the 4M Technic Lever that has a notch in it, which is about 1M thick.

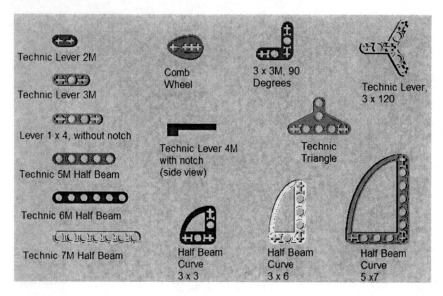

Figure 1-3. *Technic levers*

Gears

Where would any machine be without the gears that set other gears into motion? These pieces most certainly set the Technic world apart from the usual sets. They come in many forms, as you can see in Figure 1-4.

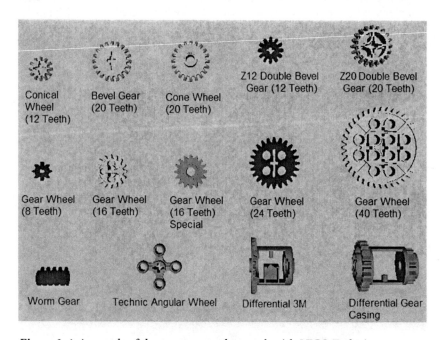

Figure 1-4. *A sample of the many gears that work with LEGO Technic*

The conical wheels, also known as bevel gears, are flat on one side but toothed around the edges. There are two types: both have 20 teeth but one has an axle and the other has a regular connector hole. The Double Conical Wheel (available in 12 and 20 teeth) has teeth on both sides. The Conical and Double Conical Wheels can work in a parallel and perpendicular fashion. This means you can place two Double or Single Conical Wheels at 90 degrees to each other, and one will turn another.

The regular gear wheels can only turn in parallel to each other, and they come in 8, 16, 24, and 40 tooth versions. The 16 tooth version comes in two forms: an axle hole and connector pin hole (similar to the conical wheel gears).

The Worm Gear works by using another regular gear on it. Turning the Worm Gear will turn the regular gear wheel, but turning the regular gear will not turn the Worm Gear. Models in later chapters will demonstrate the usefulness of a Worm Gear.

The Angular Wheel is very handy for doing a perpendicular gear method. To get them to mesh together, you need one in a plus shape and one in an X shape but they work in closer quarters than the Double Conical Wheels. The Differential uses three Conical Wheels (12 Teeth) that are meshed together perfectly, and it comes in handy for a free spinning axle.

Racks

Since we are on the subject of gears, let's talk about racks, as they require a gear to really work together for steering and other kinds of functions. Figure 1-5 shows many varieties. The 7M, 8M, 10M, and 13M racks have two holes so they can be linked to a beam or Technic LEGO brick. What you can't see is that the 7M and 13M racks have two cross holes in the sides for axles. The Rack with Ball comes in one size, about 2M wide. The Toothed Bar 4M is made to be linked to studded LEGO pieces.

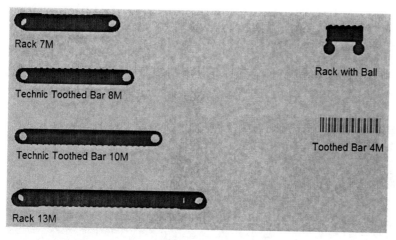

Figure 1-5. Samples of different LEGO Technic racks

Axles

Axles come in many different sizes, as you can see in Figure 1-6. Their numerical size is equal to the brick size (measured in studs). Some have a knob at the end, which is essentially a stud (like the 3M), and some have an end stop so it can stick in somewhere and not go any further (like the 4M and 8M). The most unusual is the 5M which has a stop 1M along the way.

The axles that have an odd-numbered measurement are usually gray while the even-numbered measurements are black. Usually, this is the case when they come in the sets, but they can also come in many colors. For some reason, the 2M axles generally come in a red color.

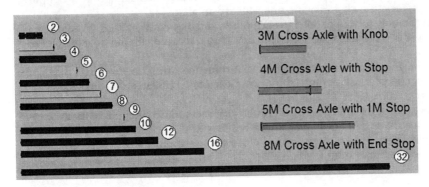

Figure 1-6. Various types of axles

Axle pieces can do more than just join two wheels together, but these particular cross-shaped rods really bring the world of Technic LEGO to life. You will see how handy they are later in the book.

Bushes

I have no idea how these pieces got their name, but if axles are the bolts of the Technic kingdom, bushes are the nuts (see Figure 1-7). They are designed to cap off axle pieces in a way that makes them snug where they are. You will see many demonstrations of this in the models of later chapters. Like axles, Technic creations would not be possible without bushes.

There are two sizes: the more circular one is a 1/2 Bush, and it is half the size of the 1M Bush for Cross Axle.

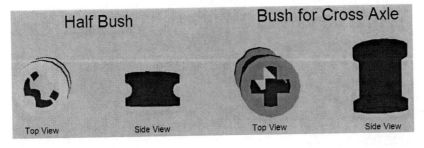

Figure 1-7. Technic bushes

Connector Pegs

Connector pegs stick into side holes of Technic bricks, beams, or two levels of levers. Many of these come in two types (see Figure 1-8). The first is the basic and will allow two linked pieces to spin freely about. The ones with friction allow for movement, but not so freely.

The 3M Connector Peg can take up 2M worth of space, but there is a stop on the 1M. The Connector Peg/Cross Axle is one way to join a Cross Hole piece with a Connector Peg hole, and the 2M Snap with Cross Axle can join an axle with a connector hole. Other unique pieces include the Module Bush, Double Bush 3M, and the Beam 3M with Double Snaps.

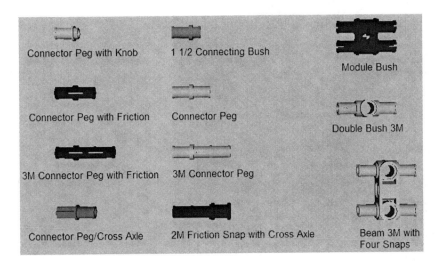

Figure 1-8. *Connector pegs*

Cross Blocks

The one thing you will discover as you build with LEGO Technic is how the connector peg holes on the beams only go in one direction, but your model may call for you to place another beam at 90 degrees. Fortunately, LEGO has all kinds of pieces designed to link pieces together in odd ways; these are the cross blocks. Figure 1-9 shows some examples. I put them at an angle so you can see their unique abilities. Generally, these pieces have an odd mix of connector peg holes and cross or axle holes, each of them at 90 degrees from the other. You will use them in various models featured throughout this book. The most common ones are the Cross Block 90 Degrees, the Double Cross Block, and the Cross Block 3M.

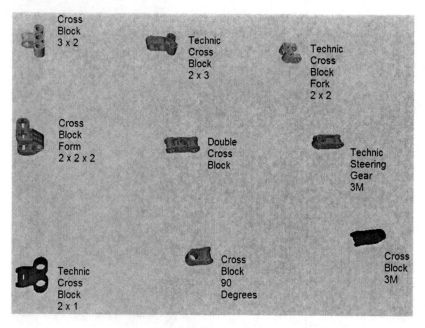

Figure 1-9. LEGO Technic cross blocks

Angle Elements

Angle elements are essentially a way of linking two axle pieces together at a certain angle. Each one is a different angle, and they have a numerical designation printed on them (but this isn't visible in Figure 1-10).

1. 0 Degrees

2. 180 Degrees

3. 157.5 Degrees

4. 135 Degrees

5. 112.5 Degrees

6. 90 Degrees

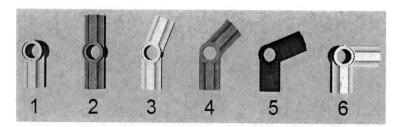

Figure 1-10. Various samples of angle pieces. Note that the number designates a certain angle.

With Angle Elements, you can make all kinds of designs at various angles. For example, if you have eight #4 angle pieces and eight 2M axles, you can make a perfect octagon. If you have sixteen #5 pieces and 16 axles of identical measurement, you can link them together to form something that almost resembles a perfect circle. If you don't believe me, try it.

Steering Pieces

I don't really know how to classify the steering pieces (see Figure 1-11), but they come into play in Chapter 3. You will need them if you want to build a car with some suspension.

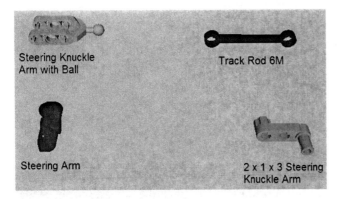

Figure 1-11. Technic pieces used for steering

Panels

These panels are essentially large pieces that can fill up a lot of space, but they add a realistic looks to your LEGO Technic model. A lot of them are wing-shaped; the wing-shaped ones have a number that is actually on the part itself (like the angle elements).

In addition to these wing-shaped panel pieces, LEGO Technic also has several panels and frames that take up a lot of space but are very handy as they have through-holes for connector pegs and axles on all sides.

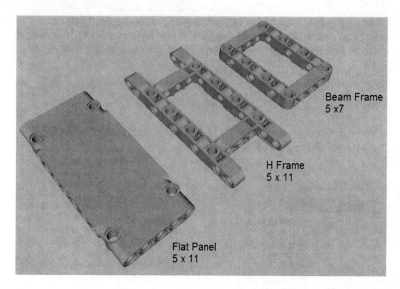

Figure 1-12. Examples of panels and beam frames in LEGO Technic

Extensions, Catches, and Other Miscellaneous Technic Pieces

The extensions link two axles together. Of the two types, the one with ribs holds the two axles together more firmly. A standard Catch is just an axle with a cross hole attached to the end, and the catch with the cross hole has a Bush attached in lieu of the axle. The Change-Over Catch is an excellent piece with some interesting features. The Toggle Joint is a way of joining two axles together at an angle you select, provided there is a connector peg in the through-hole. The Universal Joint is a very handy piece as it allows an axle to freely spin and bend at any angle, provided it is less than 90 degrees. See Figure 1-13.

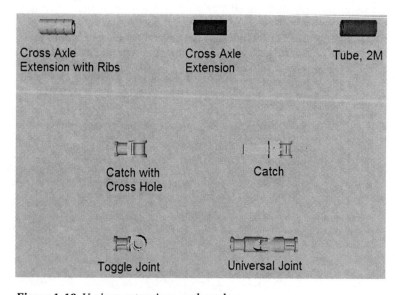

Figure 1-13. Various extensions and catches

Obtaining LEGO Pieces for Your Models

In your current LEGO collection you may find every piece that you need to build some of these models. If not, then it becomes a matter of improvising. I will show you that there are several ways of doing any one thing in Technic. If you can't do it with the pieces that you have, I highly recommend finding another way of doing it. For example, if you do not have a beam frame, you might be able to construct what you need with some beams and a few cross blocks.

Pick a Brick is one way of getting Technic pieces for specific LEGO projects, but it is not an exhaustive catalog. In other words, you will probably find that it doesn't have every piece you require, even though you know the proper name or element ID. I also recommend using BrickLink, an unofficial LEGO site that has an extensive catalog so you can order pieces or even sets. Speaking of sets, Peeron and Brickfactory are two other sites you may find helpful if you want to build a particular LEGO set that existed in the past.

LEGO Pick a Brick

If you are like me, then you have arbitrarily named your LEGO pieces over the years. I remember playing with my sister and asking if she had any "black flat one-by-twos" or "blue two-by-fours." After a while, you start to develop a language to describe pieces, but it may be difficult for an outsider to translate.

Let me give you another example. I once worked at a factory that made integrated circuit boards. One of the reasons I liked the work was that it reminded me of building with LEGO; the electric components were often very colorful and had to be placed on a green circuit board reminiscent of a LEGO baseplate. As you may have guessed, it was necessary to give each of the thousands of electrical components a specific identifying number just so we could keep them in some sort of order. The company decided to give the components a seven-digit number that was kind of like a phone number. The first three digits designated the type of part (resistor, capacitor, diode, transformer, or other). The last four digits represented the specific type of part from that group (for example, all the resistors had a different number that also signified its number of Ohms, the unit of resistance).

In the same manner, every LEGO piece has an official name and number as designated by the company. You can go on the LEGO site and purchase individual LEGO bricks just like you can purchase sets.

The official LEGO site (`http://shop.LEGO.com/en-US/Pick-A-Brick-ByTheme`) lets you pick your LEGO order piece by piece. The brick search window allows you to choose a category. The categories range from accessories to windows and doors. I won't bother listing the many categories, but there are eight pages in the Technic category. You can also do a search by color (black, blue, green, grey, orange-brown, purple, red, white, and yellow). The category and color family are mutually exclusive choices. In other words, you cannot pick "Technic" as the category and "Grey" as the color and see a list of all the grey Technic pieces available; you must pick "Technic" or "grey." Yeah, someone should probably do something about that, and I hope it's fixed before you read this.

From here, it's like going to the hardware store and collecting nails, screws, and other parts that you need for a construction job. When you find the piece you require, click the "Add To Bag" button and it will automatically appear in the "Brick Bag" column. If you want more than one of this type of piece, then simply type the amount you desire. Deleting an order is as simple as clicking the "X Remove" option. To negate the whole order, click "X Remove All" on the bottom.

Clicking the "Update Bag" button allows you to add these parts to your shopping cart. If I want to see your shopping cart, you can click that button and see your order. Keep in mind that you must set up a LEGO account on the site to make this happen, so, as they say on infomercials, have your credit card ready.

If you are looking for a specific brick, you can do an advanced search using the brick name, which is the formal name for the brick. I found that it produced mixed results. You can also search by element ID, design ID, and exact color. To get more information on a piece, simply select it to reveal the details. Also listed are several categories, which include the following:

- Color Family: This is broad term for the color of the piece, which is not the same as the exact color.

- Exact Color: This is the exact color of this piece, as LEGO pieces come in different shades of some colors. For example, LEGO pieces come in various shades of gray, and this will show if it is Dark Stone Gray or Medium Stone Gray.

- Category: As explained above, this is a broad definition of the type of LEGO brick.

- Element ID: This number is different for every LEGO piece. Two identical shapes of bricks with two different colors will have different element ID numbers.

- Design ID: This number is the identical for two LEGO pieces that have the same shape, but may be of different colors.

- Price: The cost per item.

You can always go back to the chart. Do not try to go back on your browser, as it will just go to whatever page you were looking for before the LEGO Pick a Brick site. You can also add to your bag from this section. Another feature worth noting is that you can find the same color of piece by hitting the "All bricks in same color," which can open up quite a list of bricks in the same color of your selection. If you hit the "Same Brick in All Colors," you can get the same shape of piece in multiple colors.

BrickLink

Another source for LEGO Technic pieces is BrickLink (www.bricklink.com). BrickLink is an unofficial LEGO marketplace, and it is often referred to as the "eBay of LEGO" (see Figure 1-14). If you want to buy or sell LEGO sets, new and used, this is the online place to shop.

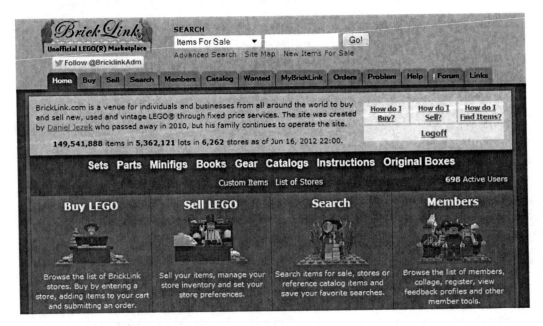

Figure 1-14. The BrickLink home page

Click "Buy" to find sets, books, gear, catalogs, and parts. At the time of writing, there are over 116 million parts available for purchase. Selecting "Parts" will result in a category tree that branches out into several types of pieces. There are 16 sub-categories for Technic including:

- Axle: Anything that is an axle or has an axle attachment.

- Brick: Any Technic brick shown in Figure 1-1 (and some I didn't show).

- Connector: This is an umbrella term that refers to angle elements and cross blocks.

- Disk: These are disk-shaped pieces that I did not describe because I don't use any in this book and I don't really see them in recent sets.

- Figure Accessory: At one point in time, Technic had figures that were to the scale of the Technic vehicles. They don't make them anymore, but here is where you can find accessories like helmets and feet.

- Flex Cable: Some Technic sets have a flexible cable that helps to create a more curvaceous shape. If you're interested in this piece, here is a place to find it.

- Gear: A source for the parts listed in Figure 1-4.

- Liftarm: This refers to pieces like beams and levers, and all of their variations.

- Liftarm, Decorated: This refers to pieces that have stickers or printed graphics on them.

- Link: A good example of a piece like this would be the track rod shown in Figure 1-11.

- Panel: Like the examples in Figure 1-12, plus more.

- Panel, Decorated: Also like the pieces in Figure 1-12, but these often have stickers or some type of graphics on them.

- Pin: This is where you will find various types of connector pegs.

- Plate: These are flat bricks with Technic holes in them. I didn't discuss them and don't use any in this book.

- Shock Absorber: I discuss these pieces in Chapter 5.

- Steering: These parts are shown in Figure 1-11.

Looking for parts is very similar to Pick a Brick in that you can assemble your parts in a shopping cart and then check out when you are ready. I found that their catalog is a little more extensive and easier to search through when looking for a specific piece. Also, you may be able to get a deal on pieces if you buy them in bulk. If you are looking to build one of the models in this book and want to purchase every piece for it, this is one place to go.

You can also purchase the sets from BrickLink, but if you only need instructions or are looking for a specific Technic set, I recommend two particular sites: Peeron and Brickfactory.

Web Sites for LEGO Instructions: Peeron and Brickfactory

If you are interested in building specific LEGO sets that may not be on the market anymore, I highly recommend that you go to a site that contains both LEGO catalogs and instructions. I found that Peeron (www.peeron.com) is especially helpful with its database of LEGO sets and catalogs (see Figure 1-15).

Unfortunately, Peeron's inventory only goes up to the 2008 collections (to this writing) and they often took very long to load.

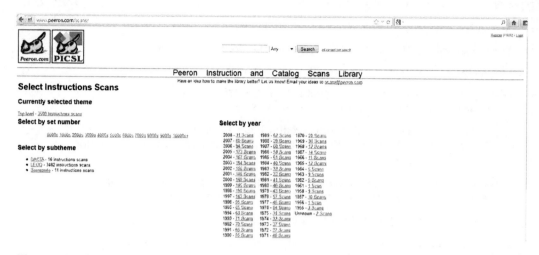

Figure 1-15. Go to www.peeron.com/scans for LEGO set instructions from LEGO's beginning to 2008.

I also found Brickfactory (http://www.brickfactory.info/) to be helpful and it does have some of the more recent collections (see Figure 1-16). Even the latest Technic models on www.LEGO.com have their sets available online and available for viewing so you should have no problem building whatever models they have, provided you have all the pieces (or an ability to improvise).

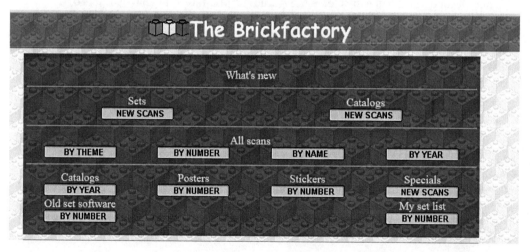

Figure 1-16. You will find many scans of LEGO set instructions and catalogs at www.brickfactory.com.

On either site, I highly recommend searching the catalog if you are looking for old Technic LEGO instructions. Generally, LEGO Technic sets are given a number in the 8000 range or higher, with the exception of the 900 series (from the beginning in 1977). Several model series like Bionicle are filed under the same umbrella as advanced Technic sets.

Many of the models in Peeron and BrickFactory have most of their pieces available on Pick a Brick. Peeron is especially good at cataloguing the individual pieces of a set; a search for any set will reveal the individual pieces, including their individual element ID. For example, you can see Technic set 8002 from the year 2000 with a complete list of all of its parts). Unfortunately, you may discover that the element ID on Peeron, BrickLink, or whatever site is not a perfect match to the element ID on Pick a Brick. Also, a lot of LEGO instruction booklets show all the pieces on a single page, but this is only for recent sets available on their current catalog. You can even download these instructions as PDF files for viewing in Adobe Reader. If you want to make something that was not "new this year," check on Peeron and BrickFactory, and order the parts on Pick a Brick or BrickLink if you can.

I would have to say that there is no "ultimate set" of Technic. The current selection in their catalog is for individual models, and some have many of one part but not so many of another part. If you're not interested in spending too much money on LEGO, you'll learn to adapt using the pieces that you have. Most LEGO enthusiasts simply build from whatever parts they have from particular sets that they bought in the past.

I suggest that you find a way to keep your pieces organized, as you will waste a lot of time rummaging through a pile looking for that piece that you need so you can move on to the next step. I recommend buying some kind of tackle box because the little drawers and storage containers are good at keeping pieces separate from each other. Of course, you may not want this type of organization, and that is fine. The important thing is that you are having fun.

Using Computer Graphics to Create LEGO Technic Models

You may have noticed that some of the illustrations throughout this book have been rendered to look like LEGO instructions. This was done because I did not feel a need to photograph my models as they were being assembled, and I found it much easier to use computer graphics to build the model. Granted, this may not be for everyone. If you are more comfortable getting out pieces and trying to assemble a model yourself, don't let me get in your way. There are some advantages and disadvantages of working in 3D.

Advantages of Building a Model in a Digital LEGO Program

- You can see whether or not what you are planning will actually work in reality. I once created a model of a hood that actually pops open by pulling a lever. I found that it works just as well in a 3D digital world as it does as an actual model.

- If you want to rebuild a section that is hard to access in a real model, you can just delete the section instead of having to take apart other sections of your model just to get to it. This way, you can know whether or not your rebuild will work beforehand.

- You never have to worry about running out of pieces, even though you may have a hard time find a certain piece in the LEGO pieces database.

- You don't have to worry about your pieces not being the right color, as you can simply change the color with a few mouse clicks.

Disadvantages of Building a Model in a Digital LEGO Program

- You can often do things in a 3D model that won't work in reality. For example, I built a model where I linked seven 3M beams together with a 7M axle. It worked perfectly on the digital designer, but when I built the physical model, the 7M axle kept falling out because it wasn't properly secured. Apparently, 3D modeling programs are not aware of real-life scenarios like gravity.

- If you don't have much experience working with 3D graphics, it can be tedious. I find that the more I work with 3D programs, the easier it gets. However, there is always that frustration factor when working with something new, and 3D graphics can be a deal breaker as you learn how to deal with panning an image and thinking in 3D rather than 2D space.

- The 3D world is full of absolutes and exacts. The "garbage in, garbage out" rule applies well to 3D LEGO models well. Sometimes the program won't let you place a piece in a certain place. On one occasion I couldn't fit something on a LEGO 3D model, even though I had actually built the model and proved that it would work. For some reason, the modeling program wouldn't let me do it. I discovered that it was because the beams were not properly lined up. This is something that I could have simple tweaked on a real LEGO model, but the computer doesn't know how to tweak. It will accept whatever model you give it.

- The more unconventional your build, the harder it is to build in 3D. When you are trying to build models with beams at certain angles, it is easier to do in real life than in a digital program. This is especially true of flexible pieces, which I will admit is one of the most difficult things to master in the 3D world.

There are three computer programs that you can download that will help you construct a LEGO creation using 3D graphics: LEGO Digital Designer, MLCAD, and LeoCAD. Each of these programs deserves its own book, but I will attempt to briefly explain how to use them. I recommend trying each one for an extended period of time. As stated before, programming in 3D takes a while to learn before it becomes instinctual and natural to the user, but the more you do it, the easier it becomes.

LEGO Digital Designer

LEGO Digital Designer is a free program that was created by the LEGO Group itself. It allows you to build models and create instructions for them in a digital world. You can download it for a Windows PC and Mac OSX at www.ldd.LEGO.com.

LEGO Digital Designer is the simplest to use of the three programs that I discuss here, and it is one of the programs that I used to create all of the LEGO instructions in this book. You just select a brick in the left column. The pieces have been put into many groups so you can find the correct one. If you can't find a certain piece, you can type in its name in the search engine (keep in mind that you may have to go on one of the other web sites mentioned previously to find its proper name or number). You can then put your piece on the building board to the right and adjust it so it faces up, down, or to the side using the arrow keys on your computer. The arrows on the side of the screen allow you to pan along your work as if you are using a camera, and you can render a 3D representation of what your model will look like.

There are eight individual tools that you can use while building. Here is a brief explanation of what you can do with them:

- Select tool: This is what you use to click a brick; then you use the mouse to move it. When it arrives at a place where it can click into place, it will have a green outline around it. If you are not seeing that green outline but more of a "ghost" image, then the piece cannot go on the model that you have built. If you are having a problem with this, trying rebuilding certain sections of the model to see if you can't get that vital piece into place.

- Clone tool: This allows you to select a piece and create a copy that you can manipulate like the select tool. This is very handy for cases when you use the same pieces over and over again.

- Hinge tool: If you have a piece that can rotate or is on a hinge of some type, this will allow you to adjust its angle. All you need to do is click the piece and some green arrows will appear that allow you to manipulate what you are working with. You can even manually adjust the angles. I found this handy when putting two gears together that would not mesh; I turned one 45 degrees and the other gear would often fit perfectly after that.

- Align tool: This tool allows you to line up two pieces that normally don't go together. It helps when you have two beams and want to line up connector holes that are at different angles. It is very useful for many complex building projects.

- Flex tool: Some LEGO pieces can bend, and if you are looking to create models with some of those, I recommend using this button for that.

- Paint tool: If you want to simply change a color of a piece, you don't have to remove it and replace it with one of an identical color, like you would in real life. Simply use this and select a different color.

- Hide tool: Sometimes you may have to put a piece in a place that would be hard to reach or even see on LEGO Digital Designer. If you use this tool, you can render certain pieces invisible so that you can see where to put the pieces where they belong.

- Delete tool: Use this to delete a piece.

One of the great advantages I had with working with this system was that I could use the Building Guide Mode, represented by the numbered block in the upper right hand corner. This allowed me to create a step-by-step guide that made writing this book a whole lot easier. Keep in mind that if you have built a model and then decide to add pieces later, this will change all of your building instructions, possibly every single step. I'm not certain how the building instructions work on this, but it tends to give the instructions in a way that will make it the most simple for an outside builder.

MLCad

Of course, LEGO Digital Designer is not the only three-dimensional computer software made for designing LEGO models. For example, LDraw uses MLCad 3.5 to create LEGO, but I found it rather difficult to use. If you have experience with MLCad, you may find it rather easy (Figure 1-17). LDraw is a related tool that allows you to view your creation, and most of the models that you see in this book are screenshots of LDD creations exported into MLCad and viewed in LDraw.

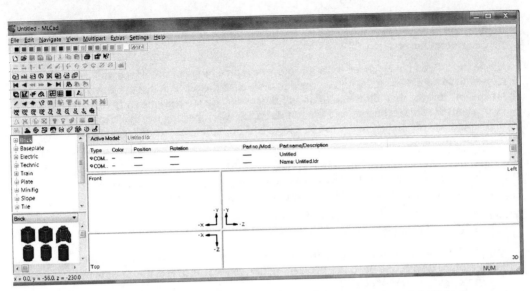

Figure 1-17. A screenshot of MLCad, another program for building LEGO models digitally

MLCad is all about working in 3D with quadrants. The lower right-hand corner is where you insert your LEGO, and you can manipulate it along with the particular axis (x, y, and z). You can see the bricks available in picture form in the lower left-hand corner and above it are the groups. The other toolbars above it can be customized so you can manipulate pieces for your creation.

LeoCAD

I also found another program known as LeoCAD, which I found easier to use than MLCad. LeoCAD is a lot like MLCad in that the pieces selector looks the same, but it is a separate window. When the piece is selected and bought to the building area, it can be adjusted along the arrows that you see in Figure 1-18. Select an arrow and drag the piece to where it needs to be.

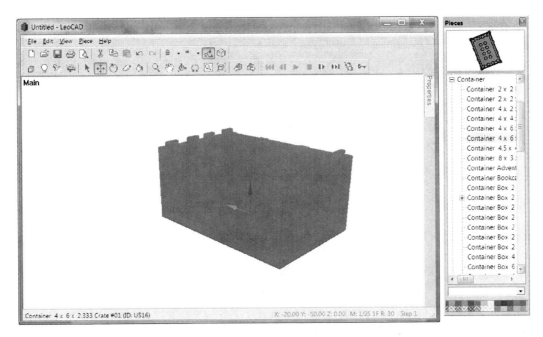

Figure 1-18. LeoCAD, another LEGO building program for digital 3D models

One of the things that makes LeoCAD interesting is that the program has six virtual cameras built in so you can switch from main to front, back, top, under, left, and right.

Summary

Technic pieces come in all different varieties. Some of them look like traditional LEGO bricks and plates, but they have since become more studless; other pieces include beams, levers, axles, bushes, connector pegs, and many other types.

If you want to start your own LEGO collection and would like to purchase them piece by piece, you can do so. You can use LEGO's own Pick a Brick to have them shipped to your door, but you may find a cheaper and more diverse selection at Bricklink.com.

Once you have assembled the pieces that you need for your creation, you may want to look at instructions from past sets. I recommend using Peeron or Brickfactory for that.

Assuming that you have all the pieces that you need and you know exactly what you want to build, you may want to hold off on the physical building and instead first try your model in one of the digital designer programs available online. LEGO puts out LEGO Digital Design (LDD); MLCad and LeoCad are also available free of charge.

Of course, it doesn't really matter how you build, but that you build. Sometimes you need to work with the pieces that you have and then improvise as you go. Sometimes this is where you can be the most creative.

■ ■ ■

CHAPTER 2

Creating a Motorized LEGO Technic Vehicle

Now that I have introduced the basic LEGO Technic pieces, it is time to get into the basics of construction. You will discover that building in LEGO Technic will be easier if you follow the following three precepts of LEGO architecture:

- *If you build it, build it strong:* Every LEGO structure has to be fortified so it can simply stand on its own without any danger of crumbling. For this reason, fortify weak links in your structure as best as you can with two connector pegs on every studless connection.

- *Ease your pain:* Once you have figured out what you want to build with LEGO Technic, you might have an easier method of building if you create a wireframe model. This is when you find a picture of it and make a LEGO Technic model of it with just the frame and no other interior details.

- *Go the distance:* Now that you have built your wire-frame model, figure out where you will put details like the steering column and other features that you want to have. Plan out the LEGO Power Functions battery box first, as well as the motor, since these take up the most volume.

This chapter is about forming the basic structure of the most common Technic creation: the automobile. I will also get into how to put a motor on your four-wheeled vehicle so it can zip across the floor. I'm sure you are anxious to figure out how to make it do more than just go in a straight line, but steering will have to wait until Chapter 3. I will introduce you to some of the LEGO Power Functions (LPF) that will help you to do the propulsion for now.

Get to Know Your Power Functions

Motorized LEGO functions are nothing new; they have been around since the seventies. Some of the earlier models could only propel wheeled vehicles back and forth, but they have become far more advanced since then. In 2007, LEGO went with an entirely new motor system known as the LEGO Power Functions (LPF) and it allows for all types of motorized control over LEGO creations.

As of this writing, you can go online to the LEGO catalog and purchase these special parts that come in three types: Power, Control, and Action. I will discuss Control in the next chapter, but for now, I want to focus on Power and Action. Power consists of the battery boxes that are needed to get the Action functions of motors spinning for propulsion and steering.

Power

One of the things that I enjoy about LEGO Technic is the motorized parts of the LPF collection. The first LEGO motorized set that I ever encountered, back in the late seventies, was the 901 Universal Motor Set. It had an electric battery box for C batteries as well as an electric train motor. These were wired together with the curly wire, and suddenly the LEGO builder was free to make their creations go forward and backward with the flip of a switch.

The Power Functions battery box essentially uses the same design with three types of LPF battery boxes. The battery boxes are smaller than that of the 901 kit, use smaller batteries, but they still take up a lot of space compared to the size of most LEGO Technic models. While the connecting piece lacks the curly, phone-cord type of look, power cords attach on a Power Functions plug (the 2 x 2 studded area that you can see by the switch in Figure 2-1). Also, control is no longer a wired affair, and I will discussed IR remotes in the next chapter. For now, let's discuss the three types of LPF battery boxes.

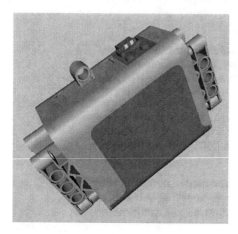

Figure 2-1. *Piece 8881: LPF battery box*

According to the official LEGO site, the 8881 is the first Power Functions battery box. The 8881 holds six AA batteries, and I suggest you invest in some rechargeable AAs if you are going to use it for power. The Power Functions plug is on top right next to the switch, and the switch has three positions: one for forward, the middle for off, and the other for reverse. In between the Power Functions plug is a green LED light to indicate that it is working. One 8881 battery box is capable of powering two XL-motors or four M-motors at the same time (I will explain these motors in greater detail later in this chapter).

There is another type of battery box, the 88000, which is capable of powering two XL-Motors or four M-Motors at the same time, or two Control functions and two Action functions. It requires six AAA batteries to deliver a 800 mA current. Again, I suggest rechargeable batteries for this Power Function. The size is about 4 x 8 x 4 modules, a measurement that is very compatible with studded LEGO Technic creations.

Unlike pieces 8881 and 88000, the 8878 (Figure 2-2) does not require batteries. Instead, it has a built-in lithium polymer battery. You will need piece 8887, a standard 10V DC transformer that allows you to recharge the Power Functions rechargeable battery box. These two pieces are not sold together on LEGO's online catalog but must be purchased separately. The 8878 piece is lighter than a typical battery box, and it has seven speeds that are adjustable by turning left and right on the orange dial.

Figure 2-2. Piece 8878: Rechargeable battery box

Action

These are the pieces that connect to the power sources, and the ones that I will address in this chapter are essentially motors designed to simply spin. All that is required is sticking in an axle 1M deep into the motor, and whatever is on that axle, like a wheel, will spin freely. The motors are good for creating other functions besides wheels, and they come in two basic types: the XL-Motor and the M-Motor.

The 8882 is an XL-Motor, and it is ready to spin very fast (Figure 2-3). I generally use this motor for propulsion and I will explain how to do so later in this chapter. It is easy to mount with the two connector holes on each side, and it has no LEGO studded areas on it whatsoever.

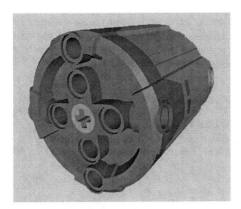

Figure 2-3. Item 8882: XL-Motor

Even though the M-Motor is the medium-sized motor, this doesn't mean that it still doesn't spin pretty fast (Figure 2-4). Unlike the XL-Motor, it does not have any connector peg holes along the side, and the bottom side can connect to studded pieces. I usually use this motor for steering functions, and I have several models in this book that show how to do this.

Figure 2-4. *M-Motor*

As stated previously, it is necessary to connect the battery box to the motor to make your vehicle motorized. In some cases, the battery box and motor can extend your creations out of reach. You can use this particular piece, 8871, to make certain that your battery pack can be far from the thing that you are powering. This piece measures at about 20 centimeters. I have heard that they make a 50 centimeter version, but you might not be able to find it in the current LEGO catalog.

Now that you are familiar with some of the basic LEGO Power Functions parts, let's talk about building with Technic.

LEGO Architecture

About 10 years ago, I built the ultimate LEGO Technic spaceship. I essentially made three round spheres and linked them together, and it was quite large at half my height. In case you are wondering why I did not use it as an illustration in this chapter, here is why. I wanted to get a shot of me holding the ship, but as I was holding it in front of the camera, it fell apart. Had I not been a grown man, I probably would have cried. As it was, I almost did.

I feel that you must always learn from your failures, and that LEGO Technic spaceship taught me a lot about LEGO architecture that day. When I say LEGO architecture, I am talking about basic steps in building that are required so that your structure will hold together. You don't build LEGO structures for decades without learning a few things, so here are the most important lessons that I would like to impart to you concerning LEGO architecture.

If You Build it, Build it Strong

Traditional LEGO models lock together at the top and bottom. Bricks and other LEGO pieces lock together pretty tight, but not too tight; otherwise users could not pull them apart. LEGO's system has worked because it has allowed builders to create magnificent creations that can hold together, but can still be easily torn down in order to create even better creations. Its success can be seen by its number of imitators.

Sadly, the ability to easily pull LEGO bricks apart works against you if you are trying to build something large or unusual in shape. You may be able to lock something together pretty well while you are building, but its basic design might cause it to crumble apart all by itself later.

Architects know that there are always stress points on any given structure, and if they are left alone, they will cause a collapse through simple daily use. For this reason, there are pillars in places where the ceiling is in danger of caving in and extra support given in certain types of floors. Even concrete, as hard at it is, should always be given a skeleton of rebar. Whenever a framed picture needs to be hung, any architect advises putting a nail through a stud in your wall, rather than the drywall all by itself.

My point is that LEGO creations have stress points as well, and, as the cliché goes, the chain is only as strong as its weakest link. About a year ago, I was designing a spaceship that was very flat, and its floor was one solid slab of LEGO bricks. I knew that I wanted this ship to be large, but I also wanted to be able to lift the ship off the ground from the bottom. Of course, the only pieces I had that were flat and large were those baseplates, and they are only half as thin as the average LEGO flat piece. I didn't want a repeat of my previous spaceship collapse, so I decided to use the baseplates, but I reinforced them with regular bricks. I set up rows like a garden and then capped them with flat pieces or plates, as shown in Figure 2-5.

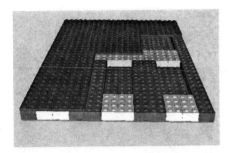

Figure 2-5. Building a sturdy LEGO construction with a solid foundation.

As you can see from Figure 2-5, I made certain that the overlap of bricks was more than two studs. The more you can overlap on LEGO, the better the stability you will have when you stack bricks atop one another. So if you are in a situation where you need to click two bricks together, and these bricks will bear a load, build it strong.

Figure 2-6 shows how to bring two bricks together and how one piece that links two pieces together is much better if it is above and below the pieces, with as many links overlapped as possible.

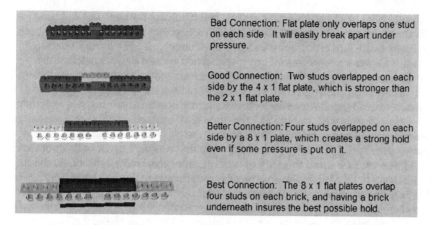

	Bad Connection: Flat plate only overlaps one stud on each side. It will easily break apart under pressure.
	Good Connection: Two studs overlapped on each side by the 4 x 1 flat plate, which is stronger than the 2 x 1 flat plate.
	Better Connection: Four studs overlapped on each side by a 8 x 1 plate, which creates a strong hold even if some pressure is put on it.
	Best Connection: The 8 x 1 flat plates overlap four studs on each brick, and having a brick underneath insures the best possible hold.

Figure 2-6. Connection options in order of strength

Technic pieces have a unique way of allowing the builder to reinforce their creations on the sides as well as the top and bottom. The side holes on the bricks allow for the insertion of axles and pin connectors, which can connect two bricks together side-by-side instead of the traditional top-to-bottom. As you can see in Figure 2-7, a connection of two Connector Pins will allow for a strong bond, and one will allow a dimension of flexibility as one LEGO brick can spin around on an axis.

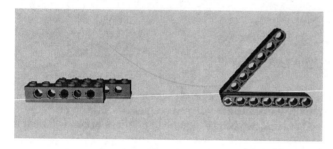

Figure 2-7. Two Connector Pins can hold LEGO Technic bricks together very well, and one Connector Pin allows for flexibility with angles.

In traditional LEGO studded creations, this allows for all kinds of models with non-perpendicular angles. In Technic studless creations, the connector-pin-and-axle connection is really the only method of linking pieces. The advantage is that Technic LEGO creations stay together better than traditional ones, and some individual pieces can be switched out with minimal difficulty.

Ease Your Pain

I always like to say, "If you can dream it, you can build it." You will notice that studless pieces of Technic have a lot more angles than traditional bricks, which makes them very flexible in comparison to studded forms. If you go on Peeron or Brickfactory web sites, you can find LEGO Creator kit number 5867 is a sports car made with traditional studded LEGO bricks. It has certain pieces that make it look rather angular, but it has some sense of curves to it. Most of that is accomplished with angled pieces.

Contrast it with the set number 8145 which you can also find on Peeron or Brickfactory. Even though it is marked "Racers," it is made from Technic studless pieces. You will note that a sports car looks very curvaceous in comparison to one made out of traditional LEGO bricks. Some of the pieces are made to purposely curve in order to simulate the shape of an automobile, such as the fender or the windshield.

You will note that Technic creations tend not to have a lot of cover to them with empty spaces where there would be coverage on a real car. Many of the models are like the chassis of a vehicle, with enough hints of the actual framework for its inspiration. This is starting to change as some panel and Power Functions pieces are beginning to take up more area. For example, the Ferrari 599 GTB looks a lot like the real car that was the inspiration.

One of the things that you will learn when you are building with Technic is how to "think in LEGO." This ability must be developed over years; it allows you to look at an ordinary vehicle like a plane, train, or automobile and get a good idea of what it would look like as a LEGO Technic model. I highly advise nourishing this instinct. For example, my son, who is eight years old and builds with traditional LEGO bricks, loves to look at car lots in order to get LEGO ideas. I have started a similar habit of looking at a vehicle and wondering how I would build it using the pieces that I have in my LEGO collection. The other day, I was looking at the steering mechanism on a cart, and all I could think about was how I could make something like it using LEGO Technic pieces.

One of the keys to building a realistic Technic model is to simply find a picture of something and mimic it in real life using a wireframe model. A wireframe model is simply a visual presentation of a physical object in 3D computer graphics by drawing lines at the location on each edge. In this case, I am using the term to describe a typical look of a LEGO Technic model with the engine, steering, or other details missing. I will cover these details in later chapters of this book.

For example, let's say I want to design a model of a Smart Car in LEGO. I notice that LEGO currently doesn't have a Smart Car in their catalog, but my "thinking in LEGO" instinct seems up to the challenge. To get started, I need a picture of a Smart Car, and it is pretty simple to get one online these days. Just go to Google or another internet search engine and click on the "Images." You should have no trouble finding an image of what you are looking for (see Figure 2-8).

Figure 2-8. A picture of a Smart Car that I found on the Web, which I used as inspiration for a LEGO Smart Car.

When it comes to creating a wireframe model, you can do this any way that you like. In Figure 2-9, I used a typical drawing program just to get an idea of the shape of the creation. I did not use any curves except for the wheels. Considering that most LEGO pieces are straight by nature, I didn't see any reason to go into any great detail. The fact that the angles don't look right is also immaterial at this point, as they can be fixed when creating the actual LEGO model.

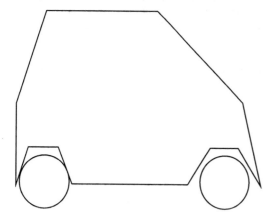

Figure 2-9. A quick wireframe model of a Smart Car

Armed with a good side view, I looked around my LEGO Technic pieces and found several studless pieces that would form a wireframe about it. I'm not so concerned about details of the shell of the car. At this point, agonizing over details like headlights, windshield wipers, and other things would just get in the way of this step. I am also not worried about the width of the car, as I know this will be filled with several features later.

Eventually, I came up with the model in Figure 2-10.

Figure 2-10. A wireframe model of a LEGO Technic Smart Car

As I mentioned before, all that I have here is a basic shape, and I guarantee you that practically all of this will change by the time the model is finished. Not only are minor details (the windshield wipers and headlights) missing, but the major details (the engine and steering mechanism) are also absent as well. You can't see in the model here, but the wheels don't even spin. All the empty space at this stage is a placeholder for future features.

Even though this vehicle is a wireframe, I still took a little bit of time to "build it strong." Note that every studless piece is connected by two pin connectors. I found that I could lift this vehicle and not have anything come apart, and its solid build will insure that it won't fall apart when something might need to be replaced.

The exception is the top of the Smart Car. Note how it curves like the real Smart Car that inspired it. Yes, I did cheat a little using flexible pipe pieces so I could get a border for my car, and I might keep it there, provided it's not a weak link. If nothing else, the frame is there to set limits for the space that I can work with.

Go The Distance

Okay, now that you have a wireframe of your LEGO Technic model, you can figure out what you can do to make it as feature-rich as possible. In other words, you want your vehicle to move, steer, and do whatever it can, just like the vehicle that inspired it. Take your wireframe and figure out loosely where you are going to put all of the features that you want on it, as I did in Figure 2-11.

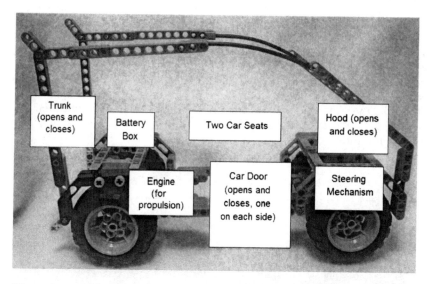

Figure 2-11. A plan for how to put a lot of features on this LEGO Technic Smart Car

If you want to put a lot of features on your Technic model, you may discover the fun and frustration of having to build and rebuild your creation. If you have the ability to "think in LEGO" so well that you can build a working and feature-rich LEGO Technic creation from beginning to end on the first try, then I salute you.

I'm going to discuss steering and giving LEGO creations remote control life in the next chapter, and some of the other features in Figure 2-11 in Chapter 8, but for now, I'll talk about how to create a solid foundation upon which to build your vehicle creations.

Constructing a Non-Motorized LEGO Vehicle

In Chapter 1, you learned about some basic Technic LEGO pieces that will allow you to create some terrific creations. I'm sure that you are anxious to begin building, and I fully intend to show you instructions formany models that you can make.

The first thing that I want to teach you to build is a basic LEGO automobile frame. This is the base frame of an automobile that I will use in the next few chapters. I will also show you how to make some interesting features on it, such as a motor, steering mechanism, and other things. I recommend using this as something to get yourself started with building with LEGO Technic and make alterations as you see fit with your vehicles.

Project 2-1: Constructing the LEGO Chassis Base

This LEGO base is simply the bottom part of a car, minus other important parts that would make it a car like a dashboard, windshield, roof, and everything else. Remember what I said about wireframing in the previous "LEGO Architecture" section? This next model is the LEGO wireframe base of a car made out of beams, panels, connector pegs, and all the pieces necessary to "build it strong." The sole purpose of it is to have some realistic looking fenders that are made for wheels (which you will add in the next section).

One of the complaints of working with studless pieces is that you must have a good idea of what you are going to build before you build it; otherwise, you will have to build and rebuild in order to fit the features of your model. In the case of this chassis, it is perfectly designed for the front axle and motorized axle that I will show you later in this chapter. I don't necessarily recommend building this way for all LEGO Technic creations, as building a solid base of your creation might hinder you from creating features later. In other words, you may want to build the axles and other features first, and then build a base or chassis around it.For those who want to get started on making a LEGO base, you should try making something like this by completing the instructions in Figures 2-12 through 2-26.

■ **Note**   Before beginning any projects in this chapter, refer to Appendix A for a complete list of required parts.

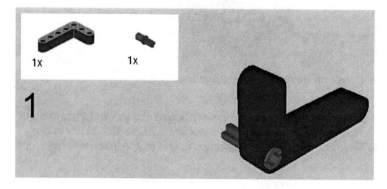

Figure 2-12. Using a 3 x 5 Technic Angle Beam, the Connector Peg/Cross Axle goes on the bottom corner.

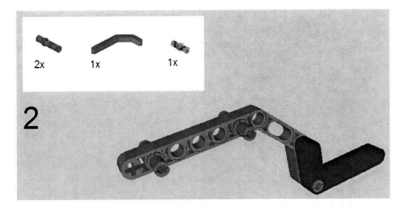

Figure 2-13. This step requires a Connector Peg and a Double Angular Beam that link together in two places. Note the location of the 3M Connector Pegs.

Figure 2-14. The 3M Connector Peg links the two Double Angular Beams together, with the "ring notch" on the side as shown. Note the application of the Connector Pegs on the 5 x 3 Angular Beam.

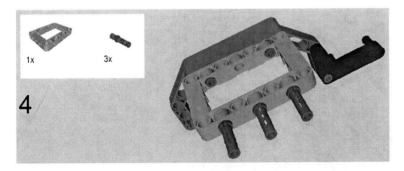

Figure 2-15. Add a 5 x 7 Beam Frame, along with three 3M Connector Pegs.

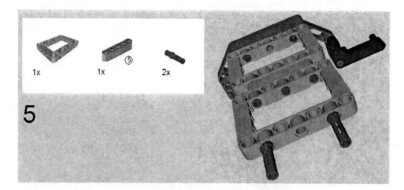

Figure 2-16. As you can see here, a 5M Beam joins the three 3M Connector Pegs. Another 5 x 7 Beam Frame joins up there, along with two new 3M Connector Pegs.

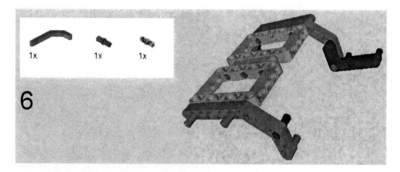

Figure 2-17. Another application of the Double Anglular Beam. Note the insertion of the Connector Peg and the Connector Peg/Cross Axle here.

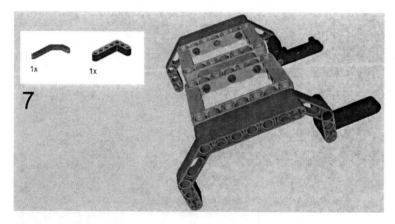

Figure 2-18. Note the application of Double Angular Beam, as well as the new 5 x 3 Angular Beam with a Connector Peg and Connector Peg with Cross Axle.

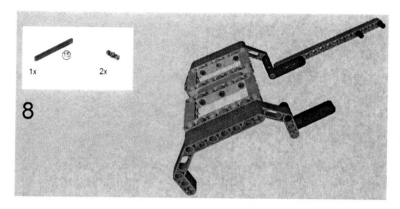

Figure 2-19. Connect a 15M Beam to the end of the 5 x 3 Angular Beam, and insert two Connector Pegs to that Beam as shown.

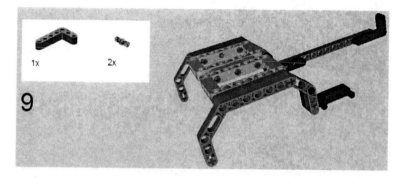

Figure 2-20. Place a 5 x 3 Beam on the two Connector Pegs from the last step here, and then place two more Connector Pegs on the new 5 x 3 Beam.

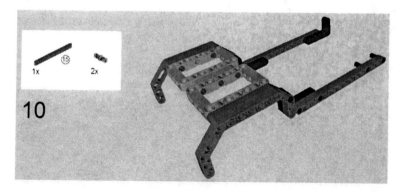

Figure 2-21. In this step, one 15M Beam joins up with a 5 x 3 Angular Beam, and then two Connector Pegs join up with that.

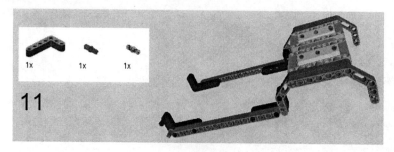

Figure 2-22. I switched the angle so you can see what to do in this step. Join another 5 x 3 Angular Beam with the structure, then place a Connector Peg and a Connector Peg with Cross Axle on another 5 x 3 Beam.

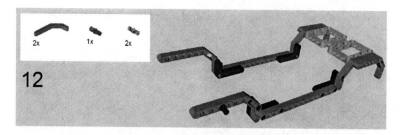

Figure 2-23. A Double Angular Beam is added to the construction to form a fender shape. This only uses one Connector Peg, and another Connector Peg and Connector Peg with Cross Axle join the 5 x 3 Angular Beam.

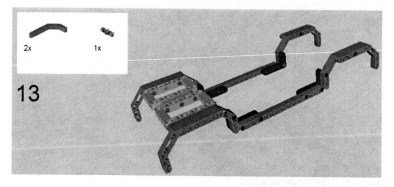

Figure 2-24. Join two Double Angular Beams to the side of this structure, linked together with one Connector Peg.

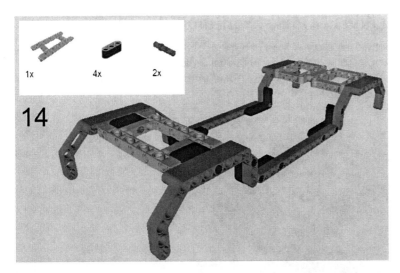

Figure 2-25. This requires a 5 x 11 Beam H Frame. The 3M Beams fill in the space and the 3M Connector Peg attaches it. Insert the 3M Connector Peg into the center hole on the 3M Beam and attach it to the Beam Frame as shown. The H-Frame and other parts will not be officially connected until the next and last step.

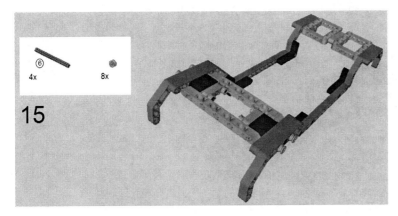

Figure 2-26. These 6M Axles will hold the H-Beam to the structure, and the Half Bushes will hold the 6M Axles in place.

Project 2-2: Assembling theLEGOAxle (Non-motorized)

If you built your LEGO chassis correctly, then you will want to put it on the floor to see how it runs. For this, you will need wheels, so here are some instructions on how to build a front axle with wheels. If you don't want to create a non-motorized vehicle, you can simply create two of these front axles, put them on the base frame, and push across the floor. Otherwise, I will show you how to create a motorized axle later in this chapter. Follow the steps in Figures 2-27 through 2-39.

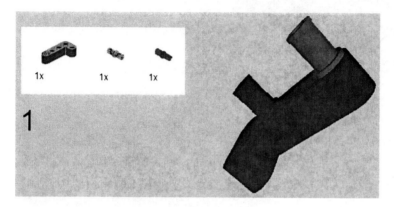

Figure 2-27. The very small beginning of your LEGO front axle, a Technic Angular Beam 4 x 2.

Figure 2-28. Attach the Angular Beam 4 x 2 to a 11M Beam.

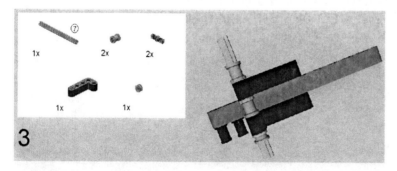

Figure 2-29. *Add another 4 x 2 Beam here, and stick in a 7M Axle. A Bush goes in between the two 4 x 2 Beams on the 7M Axle, and a Half Bush secures it in place on one side while a Bush goes on the other side.*

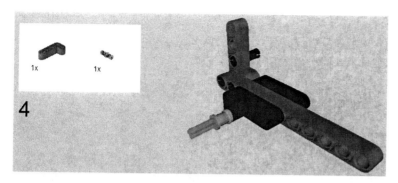

Figure 2-30. A 4 x 2 Beam fits on the end with two Connector Pegs and one in the middle.

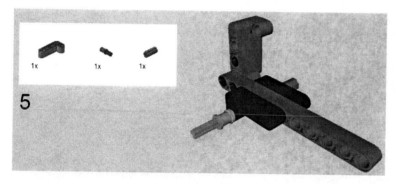

Figure 2-31. Another 4 x 2 Beam fits inverted on the first, and a Cross Axle gets put on the 7M Axle and fits perfectly at 1M.

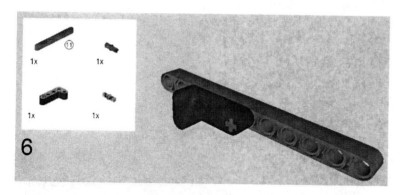

Figure 2-32. This is a separate model that you will join up later. It is an 11M Beam with a 4 x 2 Angular Beam with a Connector Peg and Connector Peg/Cross Axle.

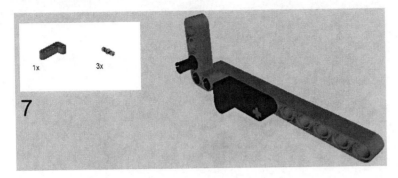

Figure 2-33. *It is necessary to join a 4 x 2 Beam to this 11M Beam.*

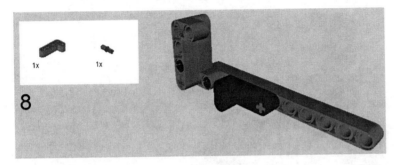

Figure 2-34. *An inverted 4 x 2 Beam joins with this other one.*

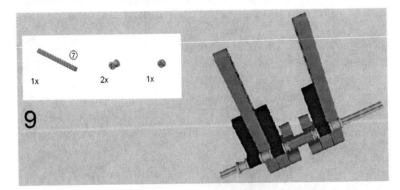

Figure 2-35. *This is a different angle than in the last steps, but it shows where to put the part assembled in steps 6-8 and where to connect another axle, plus a Bush and a HalfBush.*

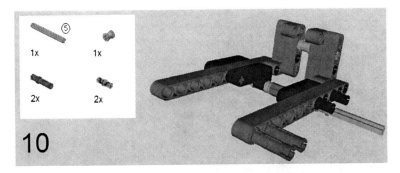

Figure 2-36. Except for the Connector Pegs, the action of this step takes place with sliding the 5M Axle in between the two 4 x 2 Beams, with the Bush in the middle.

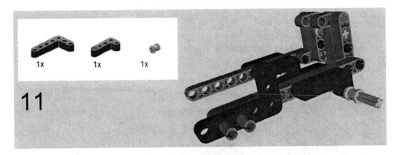

Figure 2-37. This step involves attaching a 4 x 2 Beam to the Connector Pins and Axle, and a 5 x 3 Beam with a 3M Connector Peg. Note the application of the Bush on the 7M Axle.

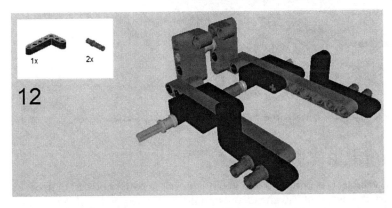

Figure 2-38. The second-to-last step is to simply turn this construction around and attach a 5 x 3 Beam with two Connector Pins.

Figure 2-39. *Now that the axle is complete, the only step left to do is to add the tires. These tires are low wide 62.4 x 20 with rims that are 43.2 H x 18 W.*

Now that your axles are done, it is simple to put them on the chassis base frame. You will find the 3 x 5 Angle Beams on the axles line up with the 3 x 5 Beams on the chassis frame. You should have something that looks like Figure 2-40.

Figure 2-40. *What your chassis base will look like when you add two non-motorized axles.*

Motorize Your LEGO Vehicle

If you are want to make a motorized vehicle, I recommend that you not leave the battery box off of it, or you will have a short leash of motorized movement. Go ahead and join the battery box with the motor that you will use; to do so, you will need to make certain that your LEGO Technic creation has a lot of space just for the battery box.

Adding the Battery Box

In addition to the LEGO battery box, you are also going to want to allot a large amount of space for a motor. As I explained earlier in this chapter, there are essentially two types of motors that you can use, the XL-Motor and the M-Motor. This motor isn't anything like the 901 kit, and you can't just snap it on a LEGO model and "voila, it's motorized." No, these engines each have one spinning part that is suitable for placing an axle in. If you want your engine to power a wheel, propeller, or anything else, you may need to set it up with gears or other such mechanisms to set things into motion.

You may have noticed that the basic frame in Project 2-1 doesn't have wheels. I knew the wheels would be linked with the motor, so I set it up so I could snap in a design with a motor. Note the gap left in between the vehicle; it's a good place for the battery box (8881). It is pretty easy to put in, and some Connector Pegs will keep it in. First, I recommend putting in battery box 8881, which I left quite a lot of space for, as you can see in Figure 2-41. You can put it in with four Connector Pegs, and you can undo the axles and bushes by the H-Beam if you are having trouble fitting it in.

Figure 2-41. The LEGO Technic base has an excellent place for installing battery box 8881.

Now I'm going to show you a simple way to install a motor that will turn both back wheels. The motor can go in back or in front depending if you want front-wheel or rear-wheel drive. Adding this one motorized axle will just make it go forward or backward in a straight line; I will explain in the next chapter how to make it steer. Of course, you will need an axle for two front tires, but I already explained how to do that.

Project 2-3: Adding a Motorized Axle

If you want to create a vehicle that has a motor on it, here are the instructions to create a motorized axle that will connect to the battery box and will get the wheels spinning once the battery box is switched on. See Figures 2-42 through 2-58.

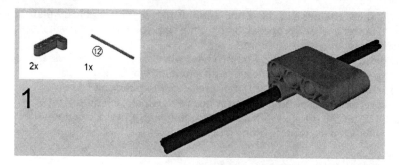

Figure 2-42. The first step in adding motorized wheels is to add two 4 x 2 Beams directly in the center of a 12M Axle.

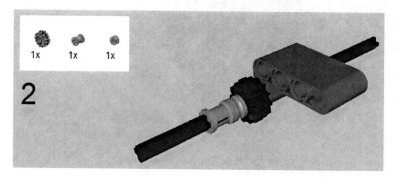

Figure 2-43. A Double Conical Wheel (12 Teeth) is placed on the left side of the axle, with a Bush and a Half Bush.

Figure 2-44. Next, put two Connector Pegs in a 13M Beam.

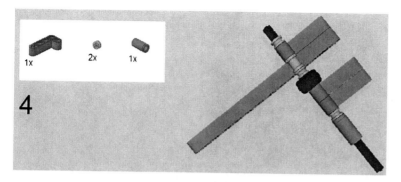

Figure 2-45. A 4 x 2 Beam needs to slide onto the axle and then connect with the parts from Step 3. A Half Bush needs to be put on each side, but the right side requires a tube.

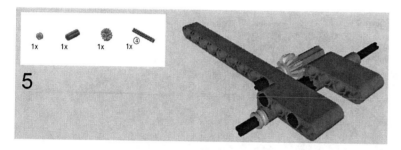

Figure 2-46. In this step, a 4M Axle is connected to a Cross Axle Extension. Then another Conical Wheel (12 Teeth) is added, and this must mesh perfectly with the other gear. A Half Bush is attached there and then inserted in the hole as shown.

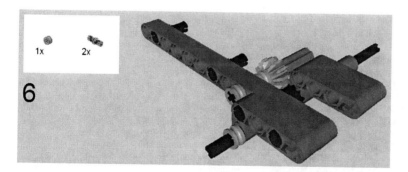

Figure 2-47. The Half Bush secures the other Gear Axle and a couple of Connector Pegs prepares it for the next step.

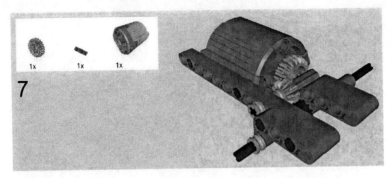

Figure 2-48. *The XL-Motor needs a 2M Axle, as well as a Double Conical Wheel Z20. Before the M-Motor is connected to the pegs from the last step, it must mesh perfectly with the gear. These things need to fit together tight, but not too tight.*

Figure 2-49. *At this point, the construction can be turned around, and a 13M Beam gets put on with the Connector Pegs.*

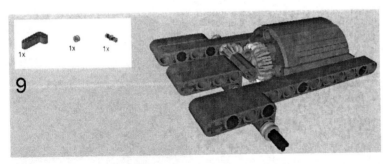

Figure 2-50. *At this point, another 4 x 2 Beam is put on with a Connector Peg, and a Half Bush is added to the large Axle.*

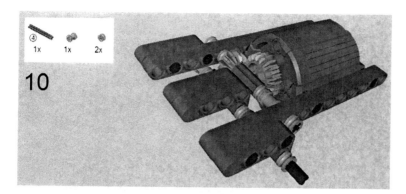

Figure 2-51. *A 4M Axle is slid into the hole with the Cross Axle with a Half Bush and Bush on one side and a Half Bush on the other. This should be a very good fit.*

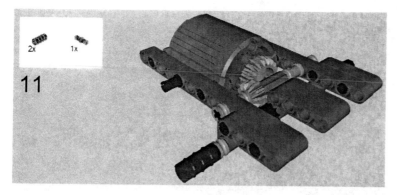

Figure 2-52. *In addition to the Connector Peg, two Cross Axles cap off the large Axle.*

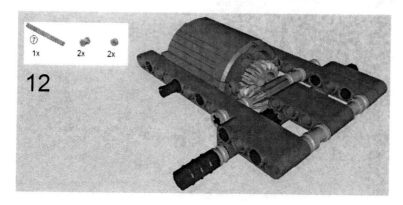

Figure 2-53. *In this step, a 7M Axle has to be stuck in the middle of the structure, with a Bush and a Half Bush on each side.*

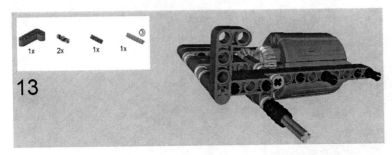

Figure 2-54. A 2M Axle secures the 4 x 2 Beam in position. The Cross Axle gets the 3M Axle, and two Connector Pegs prepare for the next step.

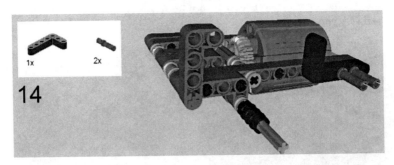

Figure 2-55. This 5 x 3 Beam attaches to the Connector Pegs and receives two 3M Connector Pegs.

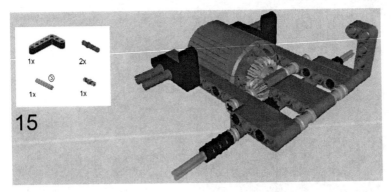

Figure 2-56. This is essentially a repeat of the other side with a 3M Axle and the addition of a 5 x 3 Beam.

Figure 2-57. Add another 4 x 2 Beam added to the other side.

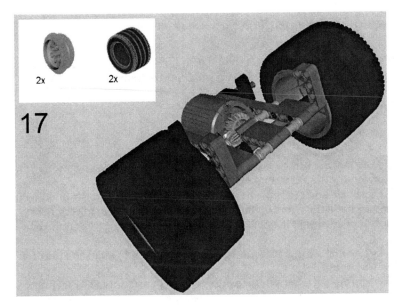

Figure 2-58. Now that the motor and axle are done, the only thing left to do is connect the wheels. These tires are low wide 62.4 x 20 with rims that are 43.2 H x 18 W.

Now that you have finished the back of the car, go ahead and put it onto the base. Like the battery box, you might need to remove the axles to put it on, but it should fit quite well. Just get the 5 x 3 Beams to line up and use the Connector Pegs. You will see the reason why the 4 x 2 Beams stand up perpendicular from the rest of the back axle. This is so the rest of the car base can rest on this. If you want to connect them in some other way, feel free. Anything you can do to make your Technic structure stronger is always better.

The same method you used to connect the back axle with the motor can be used to connect this front axle in the front of the car. Just line up the 5 x 3 Beams and your car should look like the one in Figure 2-59.

Figure 2-59. What your LEGO base will look like if you put the motor on with the back axle.

Now, go ahead and turn it on.If you built it right, the gears should turn pretty fluidly. If the gears are too loose, you may discover that they occasionally grind. Tighten up your construction to see if this fixes your grinding gear problem.

Summary

Making a four-wheeled, motorized LEGO Technic vehicle is pretty easy. You will need the Lego Power Functions battery box and a motor (preferably the XL) to make this happen.

First, build a frame or chassis for a vehicle and apply the three rules of Lego architecture. By building it strong, you will insure that the frame can stand the rigors of the road and be able to be held in your hand. Building strong involves using connector pegs to hold the beams together and reinforcing weak points on the structure.

Second, you can ease your pain by creating a wireframe model of what you want to build and making a crude LEGO Technic model of what you want.

Third, you can go the distance by figuring out what sort of features you want on your LEGO Technic creation.

Once you have built your frame or chassis, you can decide if you want it to be motorized. You can then make two non-motorized axles, or you can make a motorized axle and a non-motorized one. Be sure your creation has room for the battery and motorized power functions, as they take up a lot of room.

Following the instructions in this chapter will create a motorized LEGO Technic automobile that will go across the floor, but in just one dimension (backward or forward). If you want to make it steer, read the next chapter!

CHAPTER 3

■ ■ ■

Steering and Controlling Your LEGO Technic Creation

In Chapter 2, I talked about creating a basic frame for a Technic vehicle, but the only feature I shared was how to make it motorized. The reason to motorize your vehicle is to make it more exciting, but in all honesty, a vehicle that can only go backwards and forwards, albeit motorized, is going to get real old, real fast.

What would a car be without a steering wheel? Needing tracks, that's what. This chapter will cover how to create a steering system on your Technic vehicle. If you have ever looked at a real vehicle and studied its steering mechanisms, it isn't too different from what most Technic vehicle kits provide. I'll show you two ways to create steering systems. The first is the rack and pinion, which serves to steer a lot of Technic vehicles. The second is the double engine method, which comes in handy for vehicles with treads like armored tanks.

As mentioned in Chapter 2, I highly suggest putting your motor in back and your steering system in front. You could reverse it so the steering is in back, but this does make the steering less instinctual. If you set up your controls with a back wheel steering, then your vehicle will go left when your wheels turn right and vice versa. The only machine I have ever driven like that was a forklift during my summer job, and I essentially had to unlearn everything I knew about steering to drive it.

■ **Note**   If you are interested in creating a vehicle with four-wheel drive with a steering mechanism in front, refer to Chapter 5.

I will also cover how to take even more control by adding a remote control. For this, you will need Power Functions pieces like one of the battery boxes and the motors discussed in the last chapter. You will also need the LEGO Power Functions for control.

Know Your Control LEGO Power Functions

In the last chapter, I introduced the three forms of LEGO Power Functions (LPF): Power, Control, and Action. I talked about the Power and Action, and now I will discuss Control, as in Remote Control.

The IR-RX Remote Control IR Receiver

The IR-RX piece is required for most remote control functionality in LEGO models. You will need the IR-TX or Speed Remote Control to get true remote control ability, and I will explain them in just a bit.

For now, I want to make it clear that you will need to plug the IR-RX into the battery box with the Power Function port. It has two outputs (red and blue) to connect up to two different power functions, and it operates on four different channels, enabling the user to control four different models at the same time, provided one has four of these IR-RX parts. You can attach the IR-RX to a LEGO model with studs or using the connector peg holes shown in Figure 3-1.

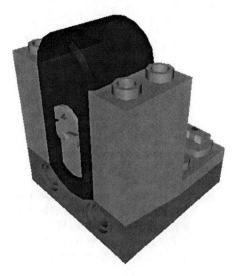

Figure 3-1. Piece 8884, the IR-RX, is designed to take control of up to four power functions.

The LEGO Power Functions IR Remotes

The IR-RX really is the only LEGO Power Function used to enable remote control power, but there are two different remotes that you can use with it.

The IR-TX Remote Control

The IR-TX (Item 8885) shown in Figure 3-2 requires Item 8884 in order to function, as well as a battery box. It is capable of controlling up to eight different Power Functions with one remote, by connecting two Power Functions to four different receivers each. The infrared range is about 30 meters (10 feet) and it requires three AAA batteries.

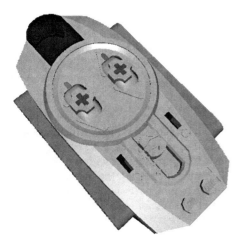

Figure 3-2. Item 8885 IR-TX

The Speed Remote Control

Like the IR-TX, the Speed Remote Control shown in Figure 3-3 requires the IR-RX and the battery box. Using a few motors will give you better control of your speed. I found that using this particular remote control is really good for controlling vehicles on tracks or other stationary models. It really isn't good for steering and I can't say that I recommend it, but I will discuss some things it is good for in the next chapter.

You will have to figure out how to make them work together for your Technic creation, I will explain how to set up two motors to allow for both motion and direction in the next section of this chapter.

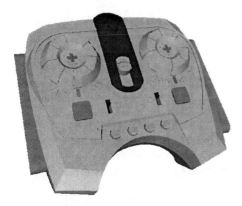

Figure 3-3. IR Speed Remote Control

Using the Remote Control Power Functions

I will spend the rest of the chapter discussing how to take control of a vehicle. You will need the IR-RX receiver and the IR-TX (8885). Let's begin with a quick discussion of the IR-RX receiver.

Reviewing the Receiver

As you can see on the left side of Figure 3-4, the IR-RX has two power sockets (red and blue), which provide power to two action elements like the engines, but at intervals that the user determines. It is possible to set up the IR-RX with two action elements and take control of them individually or together with the IR remote such as the IR-TX (8885). I won't recommend the IR Speed Remote Control, but the IR-TX has a red and blue area that essentially allow the user to increase the speed on the engine parts with a simple flick of the finger. On the right side of Figure 3-4 is the IR remote (IR-TX), which has red and blue levers. As you might have guessed, pushing a lever up makes a connected engine go one direction and pulling it down makes it go another direction.

Figure 3-4. *On the left is the IR-RX with its red and blue power sockets. On the right is the IR-TX with its red and blue controls.*

Although you can't see this in Figure 3-4, both the receiver and IR controller have a big orange switch with numbers that go from 1 to 4 (see Figure 3-1 to see the channel switching switch on the IR-RX). These are four different channels, enabling control of four different models at the same time. This is very helpful for a situation in which you have four different models each with the IR-RX in them, but only one IR remote. All you need to do is sync the channels and you can operate them all. You can even quickly shift the channels on the IR remote and take control of each of them very quickly. By the way, you must have the same number on the IR remote as on the IR-RX controller or your model will not work.

I will go into more detail on the IR remotes later in this chapter, but let me quickly state that it is possible to have more than one Action element on the red and blue sections. As you can see in Figure 3-5, you can stack two engines on the IR-RX's power sockets instead of just one Action element on red and another on blue. By the way, the wires with the LEDs attached to them will be discussed thoroughly in the next chapter.

Figure 3-5. *The IR-RX is capable of working four Action elements at once, provided two are being worked at the same time.*

For most of your LEGO creations, you are going to want to put an engine for motion on one power socket and an engine for steering on another power socket. I highly recommend using the XL-Motor to motorize the vehicle and using the smaller engine or M-Motor for controlling the steering (Figure 3-6).

Figure 3-6. *This is the type of setup you will need if you want both steering and motion on your Technic creation. Figuring out how to integrate them in your creation may be the hardest part of building.*

Reviewing the IR Controllers

In addition to the IR receiver, you will need one of the IR controllers, either the IR-TX or Speed Remote Control, in order to give power to the selected power sockets to the Action elements on the receiver. As you can see from the setups in Figure 3-7, both of them work in the same manner. This means that you can put two engines in your Technic vehicle, which means that you are going to have to figure out how to place them in the overall construction of your LEGO Technic creation.

Figure 3-7. The two different types of Power Functions IR controllers

You will notice that each of these IR controllers have axle holes, and for the IR-RX, you can insert axles to make levers. These will help you to take better control of speed, like punching the stick controls on an airplane.

As for the IR Speed Remote Control, you can insert other things like round steering wheels, which come in handy when you want to steer. I highly recommend doing that so you can have more instinctive control. The main difference on the IR Speed Remote Control is the big red buttons; these tend to stop whatever it is that you are doing on your motors and sort of locks them up.

Both remote controls feature direction changers (those tiny switches that can go from forward to backward with a flick of a finger). I suppose that if you needed to use those, you could, but you could also just go backwards on the controls.

Note that the controllers must be within line-of-sight in order to work. For some reason, they aren't radio-controlled or via Bluetooth, which would really come in handy for controlling something with a mobile phone or tablet. The range is usually pretty good, but you might find that you will have to point it at the IR-RX to really get it working.

Okay, now that all of the Power Functions stuff is out of the way, let's commence with how to actually build a steering method for your Technic vehicle.

Steering Systems for Technic Vehicles

The next two projects feature a pair of the more popular steering systems: rack and pinion, and double motor. I spent a lot of time looking at LEGO Technic instructions and I found that most instructions over the last 30 years include some form of rack and pinion steering to maneuver a vehicle. The double motors approach is good for construction vehicles like bulldozers or trackhoes where the wheels are treads. It also creates a vehicle that is much more maneuverable and can almost "turn on a dime."

I want to emphasize that these are most certainly not the only way to steer a vehicle, and I am certain that engineers will find even more clever ways of steering in the future.

Project 3-1: Rack and Pinion Steering

Rack and pinion steering is used in most motor vehicles. It consists of a circular gear, the pinion, which spins as the user steers the wheel. The teeth of this gear intersect perfectly with a row of teeth, and this rack is affixed to the mechanism that links the two front or back tires. The end result is that when the wheel is turned, the tires move left or right. The momentum makes the vehicle go in the direction of turning.

Figure 3-8 shows a vehicle made from traditional studded bricks plus LEGO Technic pieces. It uses rack and pinion steering. and this model was in the building instructions of many of the earliest Technic sets. It is very similar to the 948 Go-Kart model mentioned in this book's introduction. The rack and pinion design allows for simple turning the wheel and it uses the natural method of putting the steering wheel right in front of the driver.

Figure 3-8. Note the rack and pinion steering in the front of this vehicle. This is used on many LEGO Technic creations.

You should choose the type of steering system that best suits the type of vehicle you want. In other words, if you want to make this a vehicle that you can push around and play with (and you know who you are), I recommend putting the steering wheel atop of the vehicle so you can push it for motion and steer it. Note that you may have to do some interesting gear formations to get this to work.

The rack and pinion model in this project is designed to be compatible with the LEGO basic frame shown in Chapter 2, and it will allow you to take control of the motion and the steering. Follow the directions in Figures 3-9 through 3-21.

Figure 3-9. Place the two Axles on the ends of the 3M Beam. Leave a 1M space on the end of both Axles after the Half Bushes.

It is important to note that the section in step 2 (Figure 3-10) is separate from the one in step 1.

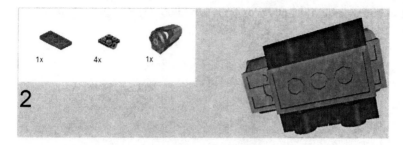

Figure 3-10. Place four 2 x 2 Technic Bearing Plates back-to-back on a 2 x 4 Plate.

Once you have the four 2 x 2 Technic Bearing Plates on the 2 x 4 Plate, you need to place the M-Motor on top. The angle shown in Figure 3-10 is provided so you do not follow the studs when you put it on. Note how the right side of the M-Motor's bottom side covers about only 1/2M and the left side covers 1 1/2 M. The nature of the Technic Bearing Plates with their hollow circular studs allows this unusual type of construction. It is important that you follow this design so it will line up on the model. See Figures 3-11 through 3-20.

Figure 3-11. Instead of leaving a studded section, it is actually half of one. At this point, the pieces assembled in step 1 and step 2 now join up as shown, with 1M of both axles joining with the Technic Bearing Plate of the left side of the M-Motor.

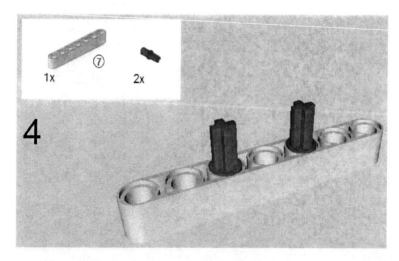

Figure 3-12. This step is separate from the first three steps and requires a 7M Beam as well as a two Connector Peg/Axles.

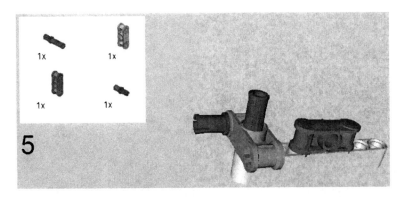

Figure 3-13. Add this section on to the one from Step 4. This section involves two Double Cross Blocks, a 3M Connector Peg, and a Connector Peg/Cross Axle.

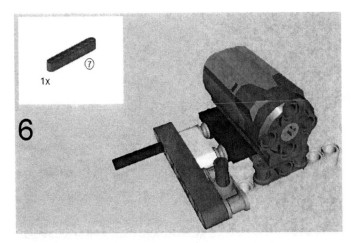

Figure 3-14. The part you built in steps 4 and 5 is joined up with the completed step 3 via 7M Beam.

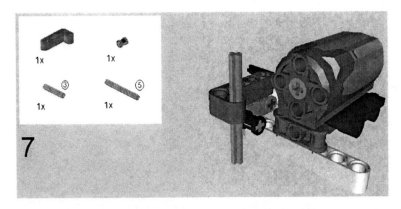

Figure 3-15. The 3M Axle goes in horizontally and is capped with a Bush. The 2 x 4 Angle Beam goes in as shown with the 5M Axle vertically centered, so it should have 2M on each side of the L-shaped beam.

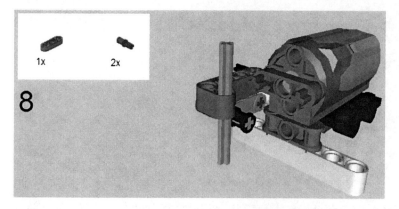

Figure 3-16. Two Connector Pegs/Axles are placed with the 3M Lever on the center of the M-Motor.

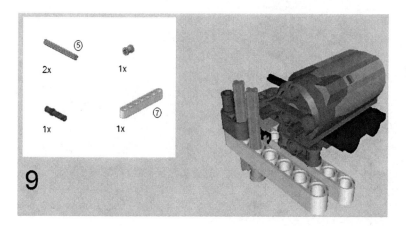

Figure 3-17. The 3M Peg joins up with a 7M Beam and the 5M Axle. Another 5M Axle with a Bush at the end joins that.

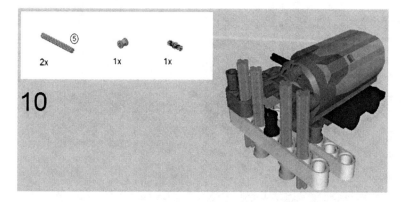

Figure 3-18. Add two more 5M Axles, a Connector Peg, and a Bush at the end of one of the 5M Axles.

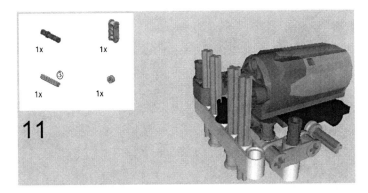

Figure 3-19. Add a 3M Axle to the Technic Plate as shown via a Half Bush. Then add a 3M Connector Peg along with a Double Cross Block at the end of the 7M Beam.

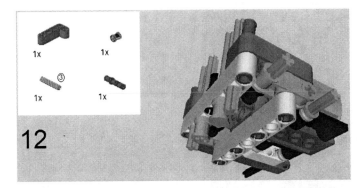

Figure 3-20. This image shows where the 3M axle with Bush goes. In other words, it mirrors the opposite side. You can see that the 3M Connector Peg and the 4 x 2 Angular Beam go near the top.

There is a lot going on in Figure 3-21, so let's quickly review. Start by putting a Half Bush on the 6M Axle and stick it in the last hole of the Technic Plate until flush. Put the 3M Beam on both the axles sticking out of the Technic Plates. Place a Connector Peg/Cross Axle on the Double Cross Block, and then attach the 7M Beam. A Connector Peg and Half Bush on each side is also needed. See Figures 3-22 through 3-28.

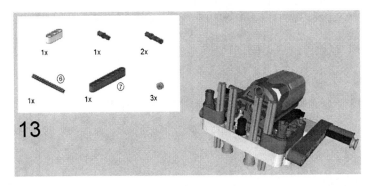

Figure 3-21. Now make one side look like the other until the construction is completely symmetrical.

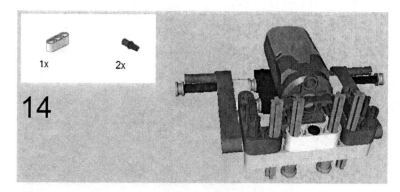

Figure 3-22. Note where you place the Connector Pin/Axles on the 4 x 2 Angle Beams, as well as the 3M Beam in the center.

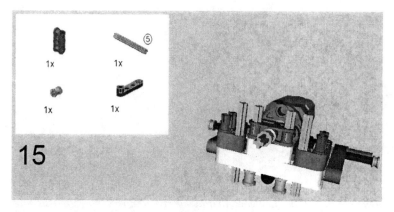

Figure 3-23. Put a Double Cross Block on two 5M Axles. Then stick a 5M Axle into the motor and put the 4M Technic Lever with Notch (the black piece at the top right of the parts diagram) in the same position shown in the parts diagram, with the notch pointed toward the motor.

If you want to take remote control of your vehicle, you must figure out a way to turn the wheels lightly to veer left and right without jamming. This is why I used the 4M Lever; it's locked into place with an axle through a cross hole that goes directly into the motor. When the motor turns, the 4M Lever will hit one of the 4 x 2 Angle Beams until it locks into place and thus can't turn anymore. This insures that the steering wheel does not turn too far.

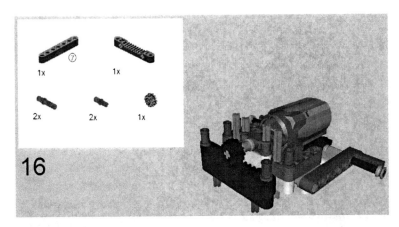

Figure 3-24. Put a gear (Z12 Gear) on the end of the axle from the motor. Then build the rack underneath it with a 7M Rack, a 7M Beam, two 3M Connector Pegs, and two Connector Peg/Cross Axles. Make certain that it lines up because you will connect it in the next step.

Figure 3-25. The 3M Beams join up with the rack. If you connect the M-Motor to a Battery Pack, and it turn it on, you will see the rack shift to the left or the right.

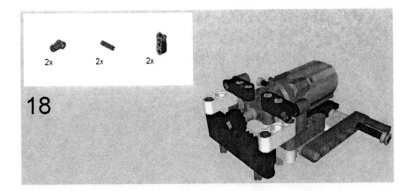

Figure 3-26. Attach these parts together as shown and then link them with the Connector Peg/Cross Axles already in place. This will make the structure stonger so it can handle the steering.

Figure 3-27. Link the wheel with the 3M Axle, the 4M Axle, and then with the Cross Axle Extension. Attach the Double Cross Block and two Bushes. Do this twice for the wheels.

Figure 3-28. Once the wheels are complete, they go on the bottom as shown.

I am going to assume that you are going to want to create a vehicle that has one motor for motion and one for steering. In that case, it is quite simple to use the motorized back axle from Chapter 2 with this steering method (shown completed in Figure 3-28).

Figure 3-29. When both motors are connected to the IR-RX, you can access them with an IR controller—provided the battery box is turned on and everything is properly connected.

It is then relatively simple to attach the IR-RX to your vehicle to make it go a certain direction and to steer it. Hopefully, you can see how it works. See Figure 3-30 for a photo of the physical model.

Figure 3-30. An IR-RX IR receiver is connected to the M-Motor for steering to the blue Power Functions Port and the XL-Motor for propulsion is connected to the red Power Functions Port. This model, with the IR-TX remote control, is ready to go.

Remember, the IR remotes tend to overdo controls, so you need to make certain that your LEGO Technic model can handle extended times where the pinion is turned all the way to the left and right. This is why the steering method that I have provided has a Technic Lever on it so it will strike a side of something rather than having the gear jam up on the rack.

Project 3-2: Double Motor Steering

With a double motor approach, no sort of rack and pinion method is required, but two motors control two wheels. This is especially good for bulldozer-like vehicles with treads that cannot pivot to steer and thus require a more direct method.

Construction of this relies upon using two motors together—and making sure that one is put to the red power socket on the IR-RX and the other on the blue. There is a little work involved, but Figures 3-31 through 3-40 show you how to create a double engine method of propulsion and steering.

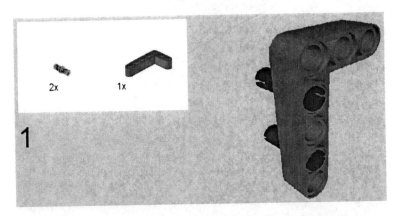

Figure 3-31. Start with a 5 x 3 Angle Beam and two Connector Pegs.

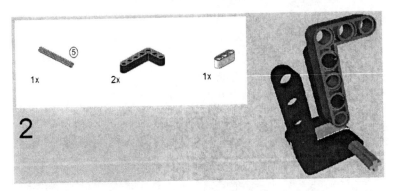

Figure 3-32. Join a 5 x 3 Angle Beam with the one from Step 1, and a 3M Beam as well. You can see a tiny bit of the 5M Axle sticking out; it's only 1/2 M in length on one side and 1 1/2 M on the other.

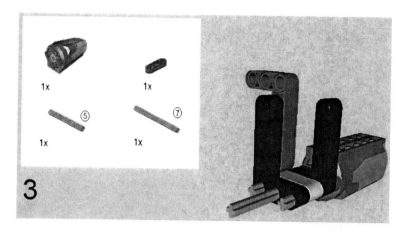

Figure 3-33. Insert the first of the two M-Motors; notice that it is upside down. A 3M Lever goes in before it connects to the beams, and the two 5M Axles go in as well. The 7M Axle goes in the center.

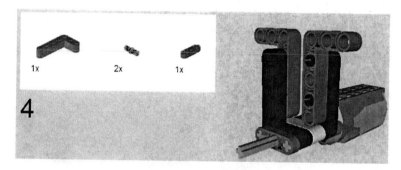

Figure 3-34. Add one more 5 x 3 Beam with two Connector Pegs and cap off the two 5M Axles with a 3M Lever.

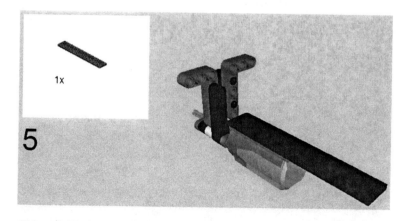

Figure 3-35. A 2 x 12 Flat Plate is required to click on the motor in 12 places, covering half of the plate.

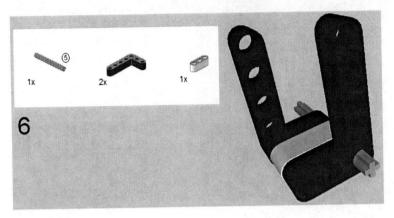

Figure 3-36. Repeat the first two steps to make a mirror image that will eventually go on the other side. The important thing is to keep 1M of Axle on each side.

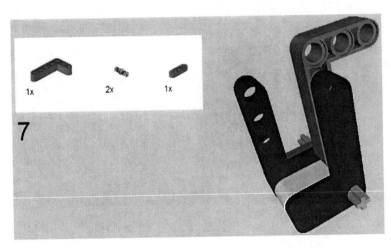

Figure 3-37. Attach a 5 x 3 Beam and 3M Lever. There should be a 1/2 M of Axle on one side and 1 M of Axle on the other.

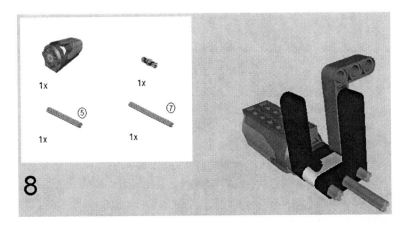

Figure 3-38. Plug in the second M-Motor, the Axles, and a Connector Peg.

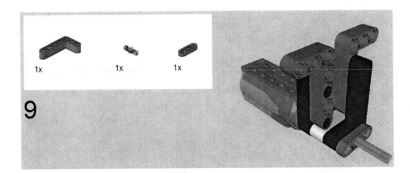

Figure 3-39. Put the finishing touches on this section before you join it with the other side. The 3M Lever caps off the 5M Axles; a Connector Peg and 5 x 3 Beam joins here, too .

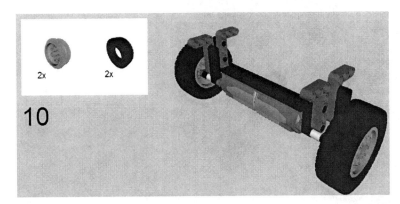

Figure 3-40. This is the view of the double engine construction when complete.

Now that your double engine construction is complete, you will find it quite easy to attach it to the frame from Chapter 2, as shown in Figure 3-41.

Figure 3-41. Attach the double-engine section from Project 3-2 to the basic LEGO frame from Project 2-1.

You will need a few connector pins but it fits right on. From there, it is easy to connect both engines to the IR-RX and have complete control, as shown in Figure 3-42. You will also need the non-motorized axle Project 2-2, from Chapter 2.

Figure 3-42. Connect the double engine steering mechanism to the battery and IR-RX.

Taking Your Remotely Controlled Creation for a Test Drive

I found that double engine constructions can really handle a lot of terrain. They remind me of the Tyco RC remote controlled cars because the axle sticks in the controllers give you a better sense of control. Did you ever played with an RC car like those from Tyco? I'm sure that you found that the controls far from instinctual. It was hard to get one going in your living room and not bump into a little bit of furniture along the way. Therefore, I recommend playing with your new creation on some flat open space, preferably without obstacles.

Of course, since this is a LEGO creation, it could come apart if things are not hooked up correctly. This is where LEGO architecture goals discussed in Chapter 2 come in to play, because the greater the structure, the better it will hold together.

I will discuss how to put more features on your vehicle in the next few chapters. For now, enjoy taking control of your LEGO creation!

Summary

Now that you have figured out how to motorize your LEGO vehicle, it's time to make a way to steer it. You must decide where to put the steering wheel. If you want to motorize the steering, there are several ways of doing so.

If you want remote control steering, you will need the Power, Control, and Action elements. I suggest any battery box and the IR-RX for attaching two motors: one for the steering and one for the motion.

There are several ways of making a steering system for a LEGO vehicle. The most common on Technic sets is rack and pinion steering, which is essentially the same setup as most automobiles. If you are looking for some kind of control of tank treads, you should try the double motor method.

Whatever method of steering and control you use, factor in a lot of time to practice controlling them remotely!

CHAPTER 4

■ ■ ■

Light It Up with LEGO Lights!

LEGO has been in the lighting business for several years. If you look at some of their older sets, you can see that they were designed to work with the discontinued battery box/motor kit that I discussed earlier in Chapter 2.

Set 970 had some interesting bricks including transparent ones that said "Police" and "Taxi." This set was first released in North America in 1979 and at the time, only police cars and taxicabs had such illumination. This was before the age of easily manufactured TV screens. Now places like New York's Times Square and The Las Vegas Strip shine brightly even at night. I believe that the future will reveal vehicles will all kinds of illumination, not just the headlights and taillights.

In this chapter, I will discuss how to make your Technic creations literally glow with very real electrical light. Just to let you know, the way LEGO does its lighting elements has not really changed over the years. Similar to set 970, the LEGO Power Functions work with a battery box (numbers 8881, 88000, and 8878) for the power and the light kit (8870) (see Figure 4-1).We are going to discuss methods of using the light kit like headlights and tail lights later, as well as ways of hooking up the remotes into what I call a Mega-Remote. For now, I would like to discuss the basics of the Power Functions Light Kit.

The Power Functions Light Kit

You will find this Power Functions Light Kit very simple to use. It works well with both stud and studless constructions.

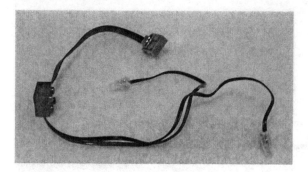

Figure 4-1. The Power Functions Light Kit

Simply plug the power socket end into the battery box, and the LED bulbs light up. Note the extra studded brick; you should set that on your creation in a place where the main wire won't get tangled.

■ **Note**   You will find that it is difficult to place your lights without tangling them somehow. I will provide tips on how to avoid this later in the chapter.

Setting the LED bulbs in place on the model is easy. You can stick the lights into any hole that the connector pins or axles fit. Unfortunately, the LPF Light Kit only comes with two LEDs, and they don't come in string form. There used to be a LEGO fiber optic kit, but it is no longer made by the company.

Overload Protection

Unfortunately, the battery box can only handle a limited amount of lights. The battery box can only perform four power functions at once (two for Control and two for Power). I wouldn't chance it going over eight lights, but I have heard some sources say not to go over six. The last thing you want to do is to overload your lights and be left with zero lights for your creation, or worse, a defective battery box.

To combat this, the Power Functions has overload protection, which is automatically activated when too much power is consumed from either a Power Functions battery box or the IR receiver. If too many motors are running at the same time, or if a motor is blocked in any way, the overload protection kicks in. You will notice it because the battery box or IR receiver will simply cut off power to the output until power consumption has dropped under its allowed value.

If overload protection kicks in, follow these steps:

1. If there is no motion from the motors, check for the green light on the battery box. If it is still on, then you might be in overload protection mode.

2. Unblock the motors and/or disconnect them from the output.

3. Turn the battery box off and then on again.

4. Wait a few minutes and try out your LEGO Power Functions.

If you are going to make a LEGO Technic creation that will be lit up like a float at the Disneyland Main Street parade, I suggest using multiple battery packs. But if you are making a LEGO vehicle, you'll probably only want to light the headlights and the taillights, which I will detail later.

Hooking Up Your Power Functions Lights

The way you hook up your light pieces is important. Yes, you can just hook them up to your IR-RX device, just like you can hook up the steering and motor controls. However, if you hook them up this way, the lights will only light up when activating the controls on the remote (see Figure 4-2).

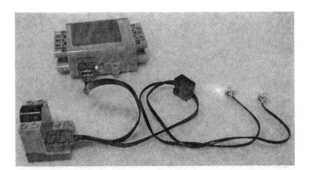

Figure 4-2. You could set up your lights this way with the IR-RX remote, but I don't recommend it.

Just imagine if real cars used this method of lighting. It would make for some incredibly awkward night driving as the lights would simply shut off when the car was not in motion or steering. The better method of hooking up your lights is to hook up your lights directly to the battery box itself, as you can see in Figure 4-3.

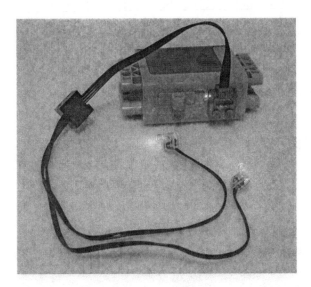

Figure 4-3. The simplest way to connect and power the LEGO Power Functions Light Kit.

In this way, you have constant power to the lights. However, this does drain the battery power. You could turn off the battery box to turn off the lights, but this would also kill whatever other Power Functions that you might have attached to it, like the motors.

The Power Functions Control Switch

I highly recommend using piece 8869, the Power Functions Control Switch shown in Figure 4-4.

Figure 4-4. The Power Functions Control Switch, a useful tool for your light functions.

The purpose of this particular switch is to simply kill the power going into any particular Power Function from the battery box. I found that this switch was not very useful when it comes to steering and motor controls, but it comes in handy for simply switching off a Power Function when not in use, which is a good habit that we all should adopt in regards to our electronic light usage.

Figure 4-5 shows how to set it up: the battery box is connected to the control switch and the control switch connected to the LED lights. Granted, you will have to physically flip the switch on, instead of turning something on the remote control, but it will stop or start power to the lights when you don't want it. Hey, if you really want to be cool about it, just put the switch on the console, just like a real vehicle. You can even put in an axle on the top so it looks like a lever.

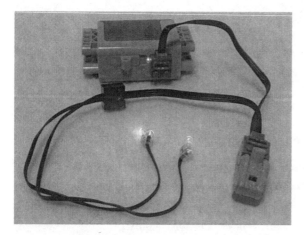

Figure 4-5. This is probably the most useful and simplest way of hooking up your lights with the Power Functions Control Switch.

Controlling Your Lights via Motor

If you really want to control your lights, connect a motor via an axle to the Power Functions Control Switch. I recommend using the M-Motor and not the XL-Motor, even though I used the XL-Motor in Figure 4-6. Figure 4-6 shows the complexity of this setup.

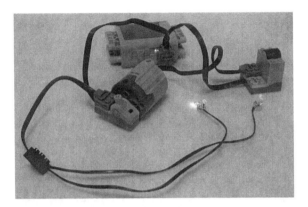

Figure 4-6. A very complex way of hooking up your lights so they will turn off by remote.

This setup reminds me of the old song "Dem Bones." The battery is connected to the IR-RX, the IR-RX is connected to the motor, the motor is connected to the power switch, and the power switch is connected to the LED lights (which is also connected to the battery). Yeah, that song is way too messy, and so is this setup. The whole point of this setup is that when the motor's axle turns, the switch is flipped.

The problem with this method is that the on/off switch isn't as binary as I would like it to be. The IR remotes are designed to turn something one way, and the click in the other direction takes it another. This type of setup would work if the motor would just spin a little, but it is made to spin a lot. This is the same problem that I discussed in the last chapter with the rack and pinion steering mechanism. To make it more complex, the switch has to be centered to be off, and controlling the motor just isn't that subtle.

The challenge is to make certain that the lever stops before it gets past the center area into another extreme, which isn't easy. Remember how that steering mechanism required a 4M lever with notch to be put in place so the rack and pinion gear wouldn't jam up? In order to make a switch motorized, you have to create a similar type of "catch" so the motor will only turn the switch so far. I will let you decide if you want to do that, but in all honesty, you don't necessarily need a button on your remote control to operate the lights, and you can use your motor for other functions.

I would imagine that you want to create LEGO Technic vehicles that are as realistic as possible. You want them to be motorized as well as steer, so you want them to have what every registered motor vehicle has to have: headlights.

Headlights

So you've created a motorized vehicle where you can control the steering, such as the one shown in Figure 3-30 or Figure 3-42 from the previous chapter. Figure 4-7 shows an interesting way to mount the lights, by simply putting a few pieces on the front and the back.

Figure 4-7. Connecting headlights to your vehicle with a switch.

Here are the steps:

1. Connect the IR-RX in back to control the double engines, which are connected to the battery.

2. The Power Functions Light Kit is then attached to the Power Functions Control Switch, which is in turn connected to the battery. You will see that the wires in the front are made so the LEDs can be used as headlights.

3. Add the two Connector Pegs to the panels so it will hold the IR-RX.

4. Add two Connector Pegs with Knobs on one side of the battery box, which will hold the 2 x 2 Studded Plate on the Power Functions Light kit. There are three other Connector Pegs with Knobs to hold the Power Functions Control Switch other side of the battery box.

5. Add two Ball and Friction Snaps on the H-Frame. These are designed to wind around any slack wires on the Power Functions Light Kit so they do not get in the way of the tires or other mechanisms.

6. Finally, the 3M Cross Blocks are held onto the Double Angle Beams with 2M Axles, and they form the frames to insert the LEDS. You can see what pieces you will need and where to put them in Figure 4-8.

Figure 4-8. *The pieces that you will need for setting up the lights in Figure 4-7.*

LEGO Taillights

Another thing you will notice about LEGO Technic creations with lights is how sticking different colored transparent pieces in front of the lights will cause them to change color.

Figure 4-9 illustrates how you can get a red taillight effect with the use of a piece known as the Bionicle Eye. All that is required is two 3M Cross Blocks and two 2M Axles, used in the same way as when you mounted the headlights (shown earlier). The difference is that you place a Connector Peg/Cross Axle on each and place the transparent red LEGO Bionicle Eye on the axle end so it can changes the light to a shade of red.

Figure 4-9. A way of connecting a battery pack so your LEGO Technic creation can have red taillights.

Other Ways of Connecting Lights

As you saw, it is quite simple to put a transparent piece in front of any light to achieve a different light effect. The transparent piece really takes the LED light and truly glows. I highly recommend being as creative with lights as possible.

LEDs Under the Car

One lighting effect that I attempted was to put a light underneath the vehicle, sort of like the semi-truck hijacking cars at the beginning of *The Fast and the Furious*. You can see an example of it in Figure 4-10.

Figure 4-10. An example of an LED under-the-car light.

Note that I had to take the photo in low light to best capture the lighting effect. After connecting the lights to the battery in the way I previously discussed, the only additional parts needed were two Zero Degree Elements and two Connector Peg/Cross Axles.

Blinker Lights

If you want to put more realistic lights on your vehicle, you could do all sorts of creative things like an interior light or even a light for a LEGO glove box. I don't really recommend installing a brake light unless you intend to make brakes, which are not covered in this book.

If you want to put in a blinker light, you can hook up two Power Functions Light Kits to the IR-RX. You can then attach a Light Kit to the red port and connect one LED to the front of your vehicle and one LED to the back. Repeat this for the blue port, and connect the IR-RX to the battery. You won't be able to switch on the blinker and let it do its on/off thing, but you can manually turn on and off the controls on the remote control to achieve a similar effect.

In order to do this, you may want to have a setup on your remote that is more than just two controllers, perhaps hooking them together to make one mega remote. Let's take a look at this option next.

The Mega Remote

If you are going to use some sort of controller for your lights, then you are going to need a control for speed, control, and the lights. Might I suggest using a mega remote? This is when you connect two remotes together, as shown in Figure 4-11.

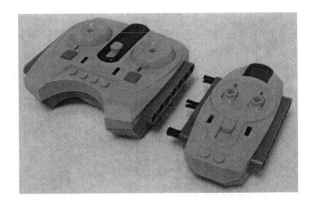

Figure 4-11. The mega remote, a way of using many features on your LEGO Technic creation. Simply push them together to get them to work.

As you can see, the Connector Pegs link them together, and you can take a lot of control of your devices. I recommend using this when you have more than two power functions going on. You'll definitely want this when you add many features, like the Construction features that I will discuss in Chapter 6.

As noted, you can add more than one IR receiver on your particular creation. I suggest putting the IR receivers on different channels and making certain that the IR remotes, like those shown in Figure 4-9, are on these respective channels. In this way, you can take control of many aspects of your LEGO Technic creation.

Figure 4-12 shows a LEGO Technic creation known as the LEGO Land Rover Defender 110. It is designed by a LEGO Technic creator known as Sheepo86 on YouTube, and you can see the creator's official web site at http://www.sheepo.es/. Sheepo's remote control is a mega, mega remote with three IR-TX remote controls linked together. You can see that he took full advantage of the cross holes on the controls to create all sorts of levers and wheels, and they control the whole lot of motors and contraptions. (I wish I could create things like this.)

Figure 4-12. A creation by Sheepo, a LEGO Technic creator who has his own site devoted to his creations.

■ **Note**   If you plan on using a mega remote, you could max out your battery pack. Before you go into overload protection, I recommend adding another battery box to your LEGO creation. This might look sort of clumsy, but it really only takes four Double Connector Pins to connect two together, as you can see in Figure 4-13.

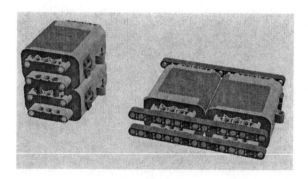

Figure 4-13. If you need to add a separate battery pack, they join together very efficiently.

Summary

LEGO has been doing lights for their models since their earliest sets. Although much has changed since then, the basic method of linking a light with a battery pack has remained the same. Hooking up the Power Functions lights is quite simple, but I don't recommend trying to make this a remote controlled affair unless you have a reason for creating a light that blinks on your command. I do recommend hooking up the lights to the battery box and connecting them to the power switch if you want to conserve power.

The most obvious use of the lights are as headlights, and setting those up in stud or studless constructions is quite simple. It is also very simple to put a transparent brick of a different color in front of the light piece to create a different light effect for the taillights.

My advice is to make your LEGO Technic creations as illuminated as your own ideas, but remember there are limits to the battery box's functionality. You should use two battery boxes if you are going to use many lights with your motors and other power functions. The last thing you want is to set off the overload protection, but if you do, there are ways to recover.

■ ■ ■

CHAPTER 5

Creating an All-Terrain LEGO Technic Vehicle

Now that you have figured out how to motorize a Technic vehicle, steer it, and light it up, let's talk about what a lot of you might want to use your LEGO Technic vehicles for: all-terrain crossing.

If you plan on playing with your LEGO Technic creations (and there is no shame in that), you will probably want to use them on more than just tiled floors and concrete sidewalks. You will probably want to conquer the carpet and even dirt and rocky areas. You might even want to take it up very steep slopes.

The best question to ask yourself is: can your LEGO Technic vehicle take it? Wouldn't it be cool to create a vehicle with shock absorbers, like a real vehicle? Fortunately, the LEGO Group provides shock absorber pieces that will make any vehicle an off-roader, and I will show you how to use them in this chapter. Perhaps you only need a little bit of flexibility on the steering mechanism, and I will also show you how to do that in this chapter. Maybe all you need is to change the tires, and the LEGO Group has more selections than Les Schwab.

Or maybe what you really need (or at least want) is a LEGO Technic vehicle creation that is a true 4 x 4. Happily, it isn't too hard to turn a LEGO Technic creation a four-wheel drive vehicle, and I also cover that in this chapter.

Creating a LEGO Vehicle with Shock Absorbers

Real cars and trucks do not travel on the road with a static frame because an unchanging structure would have a lot of stress on it if the road wasn't perfectly flat. For this reason, vehicles have shock absorbers and other parts in order to be flexible, so they will bend and not break. There are a lot of LEGO pieces designed for this purpose, but one of them, the shock absorber, will come in handy for all sorts of fun on different surfaces. Figure 5-1 shows what they look like in LDraw, but if you were to hold them, you would see their spring-loaded power.

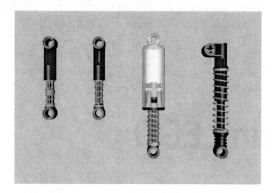

Figure 5-1. A sample of the shock absorber pieces for LEGO Technic

I am also not going to show you how to create a complete vehicle with suspension and shock absorbers, but I will show you how to create the important parts of a vehicle with the propulsion motor and flexible steering mechanism. These parts will allow your vehicle's wheels some flexibility without jamming the steering and propulsion motors of your vehicle. Let's start by working on the back end, and then we'll turn to the front side of the vehicle.

Project 5-1: Creating a Shock Absorbent Back for Your Vehicle

There are several ways to put on these shock-absorber pieces, and you can use them on all kinds of tires, which will create all sorts of flexibility when going over some really interesting obstacles. In this project I'm going to show you how to create a vehicle with a "bouncy back" so it will be flexible as it goes over obstacles. See Figure 5-2 through Figure 5-23.

■ **Note**   Before beginning this project, refer to Appendix A for a complete list of required parts.

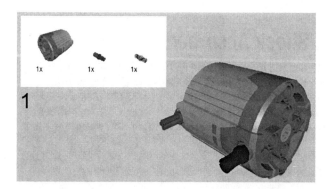

Figure 5-2. Start with the XL-Motor and insert a Connector Peg and Connector Peg/Cross Axle as shown.

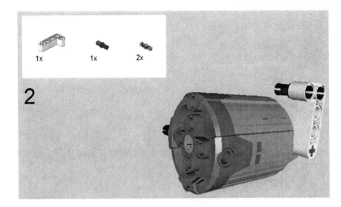

Figure 5-3. *Turn the XL-Motor to the other side, and insert a Connector Peg/Cross Axle with a 4 x 2 Angular Beam and two Connector Pegs.*

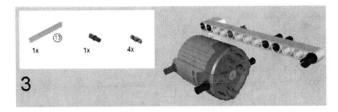

Figure 5-4. *Add a 13M Beam to the 4 x 2 Angular Beam, along with the Connector Pegs and Connector Peg/ Cross Axles. Add another Connector Peg to the XL-Motor.*

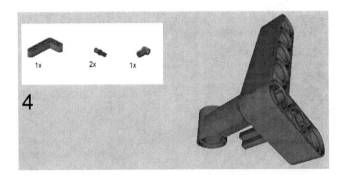

Figure 5-5. *Steps 4-11 create a separate section that will join with steps 1-3 in Step 12. Join two Connector Peg/Cross Axles with a 5 x 3 Angular Beam, and insert a Zero Degree Element.*

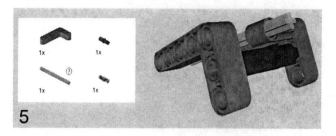

Figure 5-6. *Insert the 180 Degree Element on the connector pegs, with a 5 x 3 Angular Beam. Place a 7M Axle in the Zero Degree Element so it is 1M on one side and 5M on the other.*

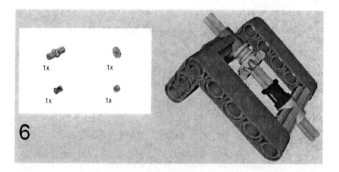

Figure 5-7. *Insert the Half-Bush, 12 Tooth Bevel Gear, Bush, and the 180 Degree Element on the 7M Axle as shown.*

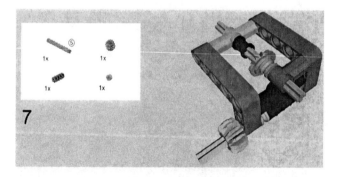

Figure 5-8. *Place the 7M Beam in the 5 x 3 Angular Beam as shown with the Cross-Axle Extension (with ribs), Half-Bush, and Z12 Double Bevel Gear.*

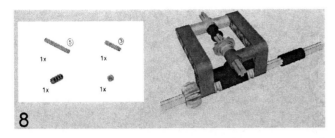

Figure 5-9. Join the 5M and 3M Axles with the Cross-Axle Extension, and then place it with the other Cross-Axle Extension with the Half-Bush.

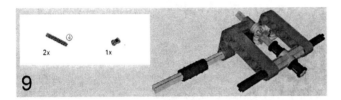

Figure 5-10. Two 4M Axles lock the 180 Degree Element in place, and a Bush goes on the end of the 7M Axle.

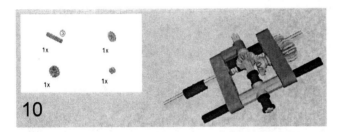

Figure 5-11. The 3M Axle joins on the side, and the 12 Tooth Bevel gear meshes with the other one. Don't forget the Half-Bush and Z12 Double Bevel Gear.

Figure 5-12. Add the Z20 Double Bevel Gear, 3M Axle, and Bush to mesh with the two Z12 Double Bevel Gears. Add another Cross-Axle Extension with 3M Axle on one side, and the 3M Axle and Universal Joint on the front.

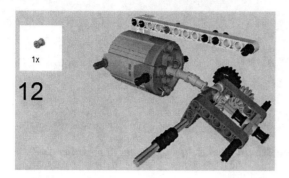

Figure 5-13. Join the separate creation of Steps 4-11 to the XL-Motor via a Bush.

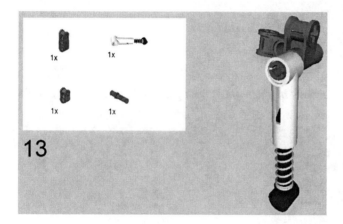

Figure 5-14. Steps 13-15 are another section. A Shock Absorber joins with a 3M Connector Peg, a Technic Cross Block (1 x 2), and another Technic Cross Block (1 x 3).

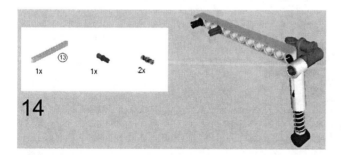

Figure 5-15. Using a Connector Peg, join the 13M Beam with the Technic Cross Block (1 x 3). Place a Connector Peg/Cross Axle and another Connector Peg with the 13M Beam.

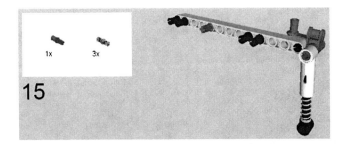

Figure 5-16. *Three Connector Pegs and Connector Peg/Cross Axle join with the 13M Beam.*

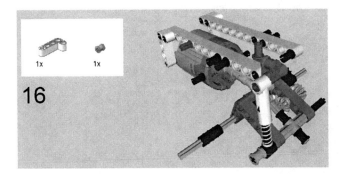

Figure 5-17. *The separate creation from Steps 13-15 joins with the rest of the structure. The Bush and 4 x 2 Angular Beam lock it in.*

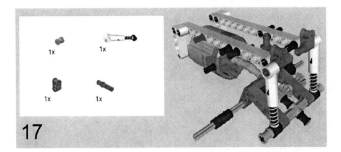

Figure 5-18. *A Shock Absorber joins with a 3M Connector Peg, a Technic Cross Block (1 x 2), and another Technic Cross Block (1 x 3). This time, it is on the other side and secured with a Bush.*

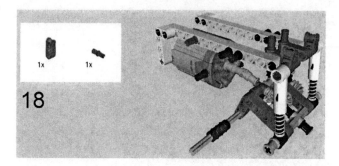

Figure 5-19. *The Technic Cross Block (1 x 3) connects with a Connector Peg/Cross Axle and secures the shock absorber into place. f this is done correctly, the back should bounce while being secured to the motor.*

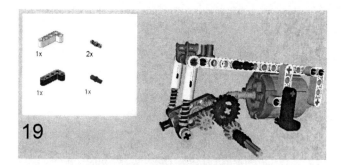

Figure 5-20. *A Connector Peg/Cross Axle joins two 4 x 2 Angular Beams together, and joins the 13M Beam and XL-Motor. Don't forget the two Connector Pegs at the bottom of the 4 x 2 Angular Beam as shown.*

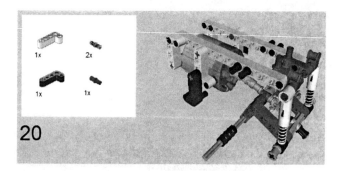

Figure 5-21. *This Step is exactly like Step 19, but on the other side of the construction.*

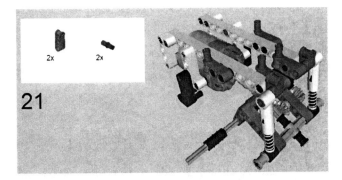

Figure 5-22. Two Technic Cross Beams join with Connector Peg/Cross Axles, as shown.

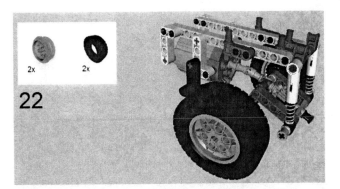

Figure 5-23. Nothing to do now but add the two Rims and Tires, and the creation is complete.

Project 5-2: Building a Flexible Steering Mechanism

Now that you have created an excellent back for the vehicle with a propulsion motor, you should create a front section with a steering section that is built to be flexible. A lot of these steering pieces were first mentioned in Chapter 1, so refer to it if necessary.

In this project, I provide some brief instructions for a flexible steering mechanism. I include a motor so you can use it for a motorized remote control vehicle if you like. See Figures 5-24 through Figure 5-48.

▓ **Note**   Before beginning this project, refer to Appendix A for a complete list of required parts.

Figure 5-24. *Two Steering Knuckle Arms connect to a Steering Arm via ball-and-socket connections. A 6M Track Rod attaches to the Steering Arm in the same ball-and-socket fashion.*

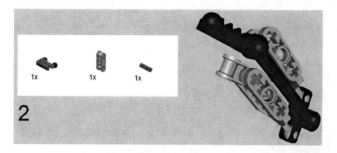

Figure 5-25. *The Rack with Ball connects to the other end of the Track Rod. A Double Cross Block connects to the Steering Knuckle Arm with a 2M Axle.*

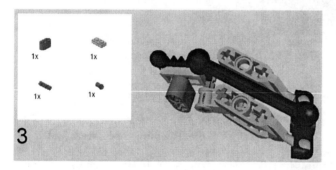

Figure 5-26. *Another 2M Axle connects vertically with the Double Cross Block. A Cross and Hole Beam connects with a Connector Peg with Knob, which is centered on a 1 x 2 Plate.*

Figure 5-27. Place a Connector Peg/Cross Axle in the Cross and Hole 2M Beam. I realize that I usually don't spend one step on one particular part, but I found that the 2D views of this 3D model were confusing, and I thought it would help the builder to see another angle.

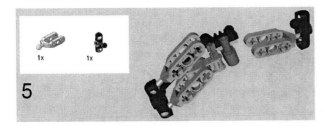

Figure 5-28. Another Steering Knuckle Arm joins with a Steering Arm in a ball-and-socket, almost a mirror image of the other side.

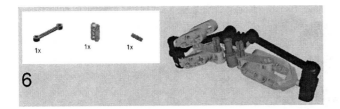

Figure 5-29. A 6M Track Rod joins with the Steering Arm and Rack with Ball. A Double Cross Block with 2M Axle also joins here.

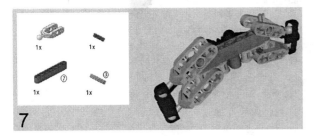

Figure 5-30. Insert a 2M Axle to join the Steering Knuckle Arm with the Double Cross Block. Another Steering Knuckle Arm joins here, and a 7M Beam joins the two sides together. Don't forget to add the 3M Axle vertically on the Double Cross Block.

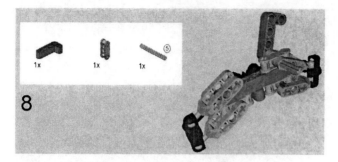

Figure 5-31. A 5M Axle joins with a new Double Cross Block and also connects with the cross-hole of the 4 x 2 Technic Angular Beam.

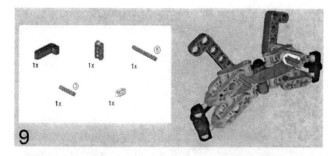

Figure 5-32. Add another Double Cross Block, 5M Axle, and 4 x 2 Angular Beam. Add another 3M Axle vertically through the two Double Cross Blocks on the left and a 2M Lever on one of the 5M Axles.

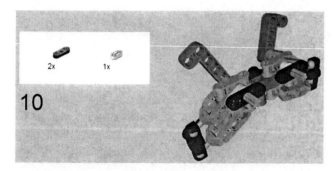

Figure 5-33. Add another 2M Lever on the other side, and two 3M Levers here.

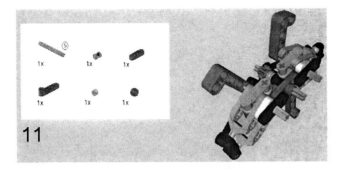

Figure 5-34. Connect a 4M Lever with notch, 3M Lever, Bush, Half-Bush, and 8 Tooth gear to a 5M Axle. The Gear meshes with the Rack.

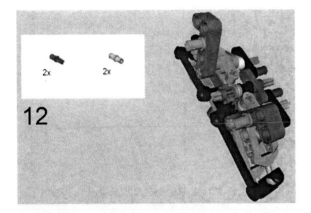

Figure 5-35. The Connector Peg/Cross Axles join the 3M Levers, and the Connector Pegs (gray) join the 4 x 2 Angular Beams as shown.

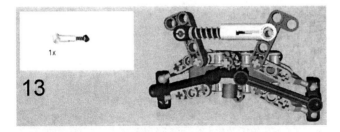

Figure 5-36. The Shock Absorber piece joins with the Connector Pegs on the Angular Beams here. This will keep the Track Rods at different angles.

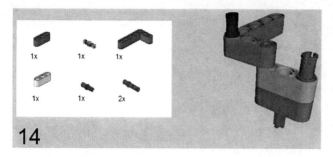

Figure 5-37. *This is a separate creation that will join the whole in the next step. It requires two 3M Beams, two 3M Connector Pegs, a Connector Peg/Cross Axle, and a Connector Peg.*

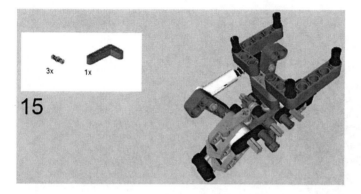

Figure 5-38. *The miniature creation from Step 14 joins with a Double Cross Block. Another 4 x 2 Angular Beam with three Connector Pegs join here as well.*

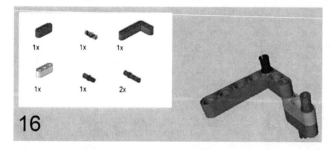

Figure 5-39. *This is another separate creation, and it is essentially a mirror image of Step 14.*

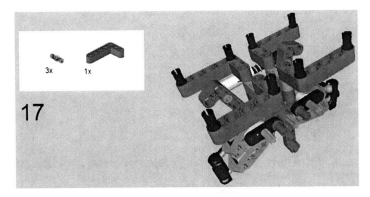

Figure 5-40. Add another 4 x 2 Angular Beam with three Connector Pegs.

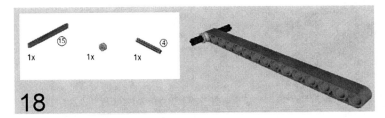

Figure 5-41. This is another separate creation. Start with a 15M Beam and add the 4M Axle with Half-Bush. Leave 1M of Axle exposed on the side with the Half-Bush.

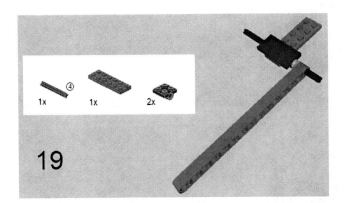

Figure 5-42. Two Technic Bearing Plates attach to a 2 x 6 Plate and join the construction here. Another 4M Axle joins the other side.

Figure 5-43. Another Half Bush and 15M Beam join at this point, and another Technic Bearing plate and 4M Axle join as shown.

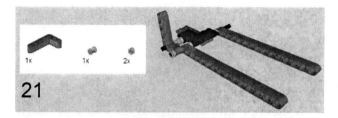

Figure 5-44. A 4 x 2 Angular Beam, Bush, and two Half-Bushes join the construction as shown.

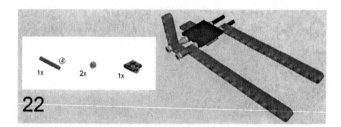

Figure 5-45. Another 4M beam with Half-Bush join with a Technic Bearing Plate. A Half-Bush caps off a 4M Axle.

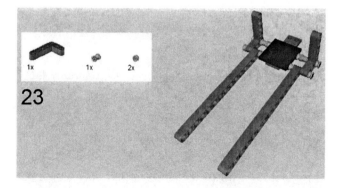

Figure 5-46. Like Step 21, a 4 x 2 Angular Beam, Bush, and two Half-Bushes join the construction as shown.

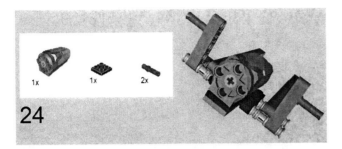

Figure 5-47. Add a 2 x 2 Plate on the 2 x 6 Plate and place the M-Motor over the entire 2 x 6 area. The 3M Connector Pegs go on the side as shown.

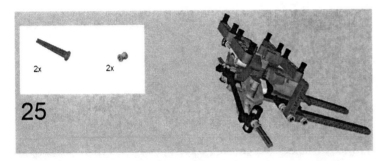

Figure 5-48. The section with the motor attaches to the steering section. The 4M Axles with stop also attach to the Steering Arms, along with the Bushes.

At this point, you can take the shock absorbent back and flexible steering mechanism front and make a motorized vehicle from the frame in Project 2-1 in Chapter 2. It should attach relatively easily, as you can see in Figure 5-49.

Figure 5-49. Projects 5-1 and 5-2 can link up to Project 2-1 quite easily. You will also need to attach the rims and tires.

From here, you can connect the battery box and the IR-RX and take control of this vehicle as in Figure 5-50.

Figure 5-50. Attaching the battery box and IR-RX to your vehicle.

In Project 5-1 and 5-2, I didn't focus on what type of tires to use, so let's look at some options now.

Check Your Tires

You may discover that all you really need to get your LEGO vehicle over more rugged terrain are bigger and stronger tires. Just like real tires have specs written on them, some of the larger tires also have their specs written along the side.

You might need to leave more room for the new rim and tire because the base that I showed you how to build in Chapter 2 cannot handle larger tires. It's worth it if you really want to get yourself some extra traction. Note that depending on the scale of your truck, changing the tires could make your creation resemble a monster truck.

If you are looking for some real traction, I recommend the double engine method that I discussed in Chapter 3. It makes remote control activity quite fun and can give your vehicles a lot of control plus the ability to make some spinning turns. That, or go with a four-wheel drive vehicle.

Making a LEGO Technic 4x4 Vehicle

Of course, if you want to take on obstacles, you need a vehicle with four-wheel drive. So far, I have discussed how to make a vehicle with a motor in the back or front and a steering system for the other set of wheels. Sure, this is enough if all you want is for your vehicle to go on some flat, stable land, but if you really want to go all-terrain, then power needs to be supplied to all four tires.

In 4 x 4 vehicles, you want to tie all four tires into one axle for the motor for propulsion. This isn't really all that difficult if you just arrange your gears properly, but this will create a vehicle that will not be able to steer because the front axle will be too stiff. The solution is to use pieces known as universal joints (shown in Chapter 1, Figure 1-13) to allow your axle to pivot while spinning.

Project 5-3: Assembling the H-Frame and Accessories

Before I begin, I want to make a brief disclaimer: I will no longer be using the basic LEGO base frame that I introduced in Chapter 2. It came in handy for demonstrating basic steering, propulsion, and lighting systems on LEGO Technic models in the last three chapters, but I am hoping that you have learned from it and can apply those systems to models of your own.

This project shows how to create a motorized 4 x 4 vehicle that you can steer remotely. Brace yourself; there is a lot of ground to cover. In fact, it's 60 steps. As much as I would love to break them up in some logical way, this whole 4 x 4 construction requires unity to get to work. So let's get to it. See Figures 5-51 through 5-110.

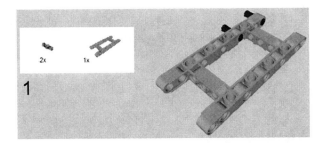

Figure 5-51. Start with a 5 x 11 H-Frame and two Connector Pegs.

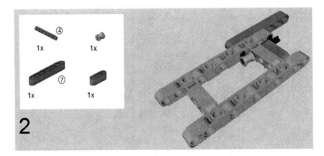

Figure 5-52. A 3M Beam joins with the H-Frame and connects with a 4M Axle and Bush. The 7M Beam is only placed there for now, but it will be linked later.

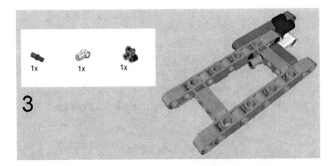

Figure 5-53. Using a Connector Pin/Cross Axle, a Zero Degree Element, and a Technic Cross Block, attach the H-Frame to the structure itself. This is one of four times you will use this method of construction.

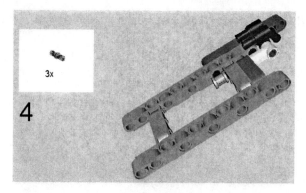

Figure 5-54. Two of the Connector Pegs go in the Technic Cross Axle and the third goes in the 7M Beam as shown.

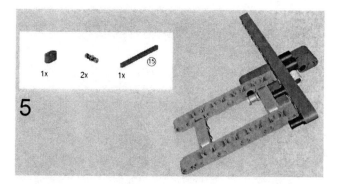

Figure 5-55. A 15M Beam joins with the Cross Axle, and it has its own Connector Pegs as well. The Cross and Hole Beam joins with the 7M Beam.

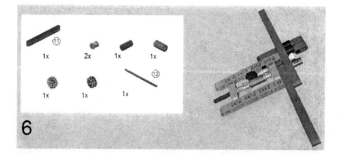

Figure 5-56. The 12M Axle goes in the H-Frame with two Bushes, a Tube, and two Z12 Conical Gear Wheels mesh together in a perpendicular fashion, with one facing one way and the other facing at 90 degrees.

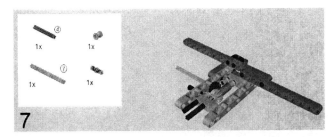

Figure 5-57. *The 7M Axle joins up with the Z12 Conical Gear Wheel as part of the main central axle of the creation. A 4M Axle and Bush joins with the H-Frame, along with a Connector Pin.*

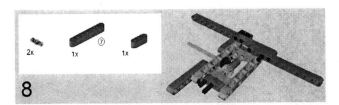

Figure 5-58. *A Connector Pin joins a 7M Beam with the H-Frame, and a 3M Beam joins the H-Frame.*

Figure 5-59. *This Zero Degree Angle Element and two Connector Pins will come into play later in Step 47 to hold the engine for propulsion.*

Figure 5-60. *The Double Cross Block joins with a 7M Beam with two Connector Peg/Cross Axles, which then join up to the 15M Beam.*

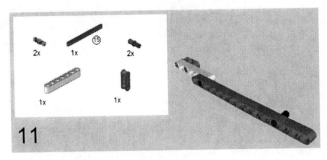

Figure 5-61. *This section is a partial repeat of Step 10 but it is built separately from the construction. Just connect the Double Cross Block to the 7M Beam, and connect that to the 15M Beam.*

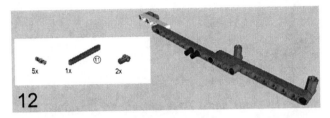

Figure 5-62. *Add two Zero Degree Elements, five Connector Pegs, and a 11M Beam to the section created in Step 11.*

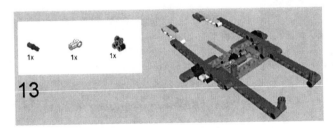

Figure 5-63. *Now join the section from Step 12 to the rest of the creation via a Technic Cross Block, a Zero Degree Element, and a Connector Peg/Cross Axle.*

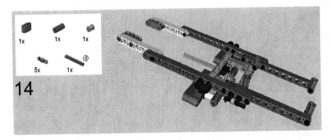

Figure 5-64. *At this point, a 4M Axle joins the H-Frame with a Bush. A Cross Axle joins with the 12M Axle, and a Cross and Hole joins up here as well.*

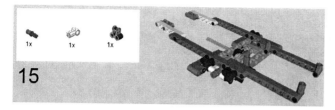

Figure 5-65. This step is similar to Steps 3 and 13, with a Technic Cross Block, a Zero Degree Element, and Connector Peg/Cross Axle.

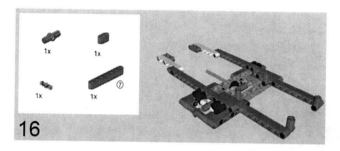

Figure 5-66. Another 7M Beam joins up. Place the 180 Angle Element in the middle to be joined up with the axles in the next step.

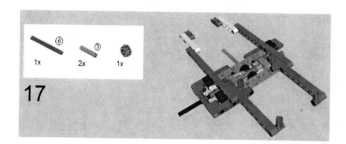

Figure 5-67. Two 3M Axles join the 180 Degree Angle Element. Then insert a 6M Axle in a perpendicular manner. Note the placement of the Z12 Gear in the H-Frame, which must mesh there.

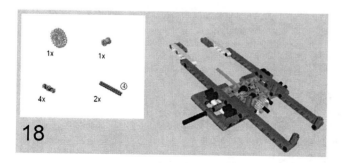

Figure 5-68. Join the Z12 gear with a 4M Axle and a Z20 Conical Wheel. Note the placement of the Connector Pegs (two on the H-Frame that mirror the other side) and a second 4M Axle with a Bush.

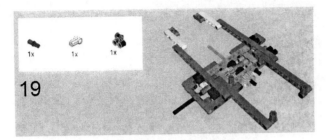

Figure 5-69. This step is almost identical to Step 3 and joins the H-Frame to the structure.

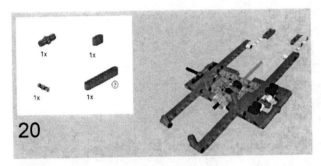

Figure 5-70. This is a repeat of what you did on the other side in Steps 16 and 17, which involves a 180 Degree Element.

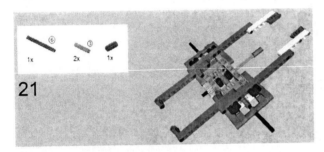

Figure 5-71. Two 3M Axles join here on the 180 Degree Element, along with a 6M Axle. Note the Cross Axle extention on the middle.

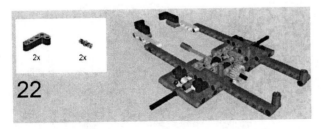

Figure 5-72. Now work on the other side of the creation. With the help of some Connector Pins, the two 4 x 2 Angular Beams join up.

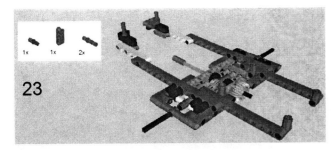

Figure 5-73. *Add a 3M Cross Block and two types of Connector Pegs to the 4 x 2 Beams from last step.*

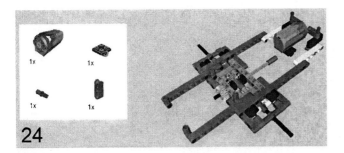

Figure 5-74. *The steering engine (M-Motor) is plugged in to the front. Note how the 2x 2 Technic Bearing Plate is on the motor. With its hollow studs, it comes in about half a stud into the motor. This is similar to the rack and pinion steering column in Chapter 3.*

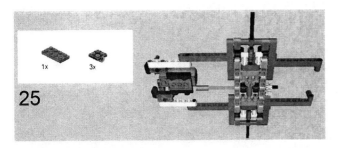

Figure 5-75. *More Technic Bearing Plates get involved, with a 4 x 2 Flat Plate to hold them all in place. Note the placement on the motor.*

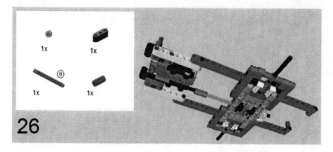

Figure 5-76. The central axle gets an extension and a 6M Axle. A Half Bush and 3M Beam get involved with the Technic Bearing Plates.

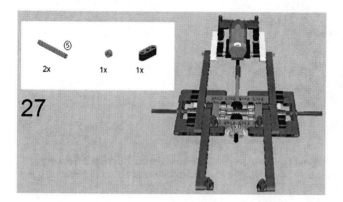

Figure 5-77. The two 5M Axles, a 3M Beam, and Half Bush help join the M-Motor with the rest of the structure.

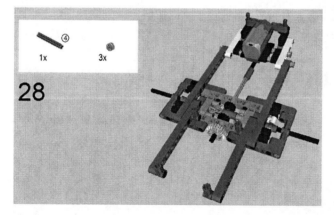

Figure 5-78. The Half Bushes and Axle also insure that the M-Motor will stay in place.

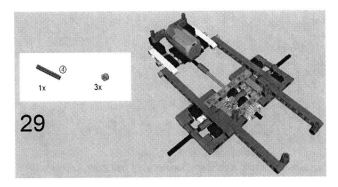

Figure 5-79. *By this step, the M-Motor should be well established in place with the addition of the Axles and Half Bushes.*

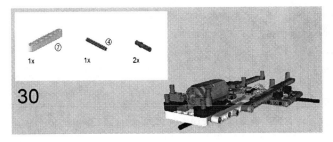

Figure 5-80. *I shifted the viewing angle so you can see where the 7M Beam joins, as well as the addition of a 4M Axle on the main axle.*

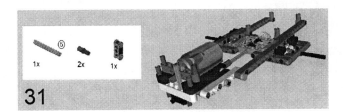

Figure 5-81. *Place a Double Cross Block on the bottom with a 5M Axle extending from it, along with two Connector Peg/Cross Axles.*

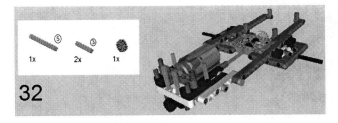

Figure 5-82. *Note the placement of the Z12 Gear Wheel on the bottom, as well as the new 5M Axle. The 3M Axles go on each side, inserted into the 4 x 2 Angle Beams.*

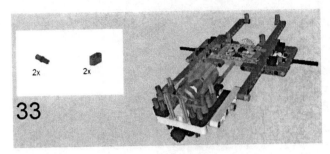

Figure 5-83. Two of the Cross and Hole pieces go on the 3M Axles, and two Connector Pin/Cross Axles go in on the 4 x 2 Angle Beams.

Figure 5-84. The two Levers go over the 5M Axles, and a 2M Axle goes in one of the Levers. A Connector Peg goes on one of the Cross and Hole pieces.

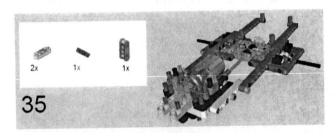

Figure 5-85. The 3M Levers go atop the other levers, the 2M Axle goes between them, and a Double Cross Block goes atop that.

Figure 5-86. Many of the pieces in this step are devoted to making the piece in front of the structure, but you won't link to it until later. Don't forget to add the three Friction Snaps with Cross Holes as well.

Figure 5-87. Repeat step 37 to create a second section, also to be linked later.

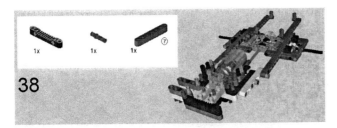

Figure 5-88. Create another piece to place in front of the construction here, joining a 7M Rack with a 7M Beam using a 3M Connector Peg. Yes, this will be used for steering and it will be joined to the construction later.

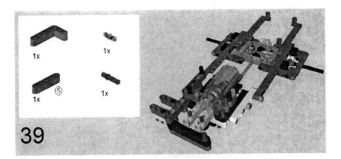

Figure 5-89. The 5M Beam joins up the pieces built in the last three steps, and the 5 x 3 Angle Beam is placed atop of it. Note the placement of the Connector Peg.

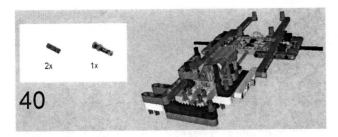

Figure 5-90. Note the addition of the 2M Axles and the 2M Friction Snap with Cross Hole as well.

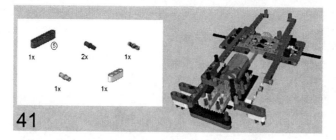

Figure 5-91. *Repeat Step 36 to make an identical section.*

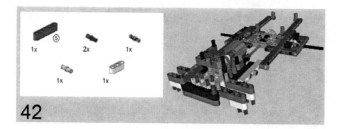

Figure 5-92. *Create another identical construction, as in the last step.*

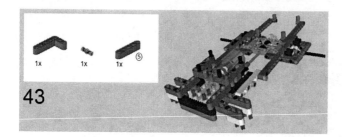

Figure 5-93. *Place a 5M Beam and 5 x 3 Beam to join up the pieces from the last two steps.*

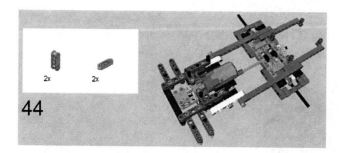

Figure 5-94. *In addition to the Cross Blocks, two 3M Levers must be placed in front of the M-Motor's Axle Spinner, pointed downward.*

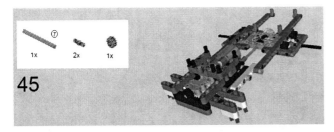

Figure 5-95. *Use the 7M Axle to connect the Levers and Cross Blocks from the last step. The Z12 Conical Gear Wheel must be in dead center and meshed with the rack. Note the placement of the Connector Pegs.*

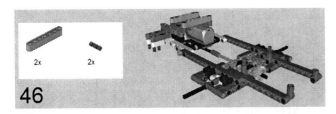

Figure 5-96. *The two 7M Beams secure the steering section, and the two 2M Axles join up with the Zero Angle Elements in the back.*

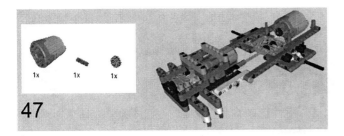

Figure 5-97. *Add the XL-Motor and connect the Z12 Conical Wheel to it with the 2M Axle. Make certain the gears mesh together, for this will be set in place strongly in later steps.*

Figure 5-98. *Another Zero Angle Element joins with the other one, turned at a ninety degree angle. Note the addition made to the XL-Motor with a 3M Cross Block and Connector Peg/Cross Axle.*

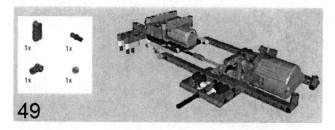

Figure 5-99. Shown from another angle, the additions are linked to the XL-Motor. You will need to use a Half Bush as a placeholder.

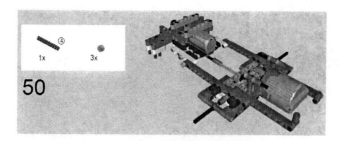

Figure 5-100. Use a 4M Axle and three Half Bushes to keep the XL-Motor in place.

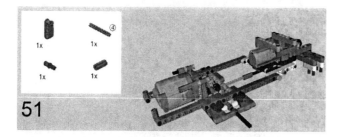

Figure 5-101. Once again, add the Connector Peg/Cross Axle and 3M Cross Block pieces to the XL-Motor. This time insert a 4M Axle and Cross Axle Extension.

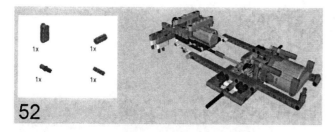

Figure 5-102. This is essentially mirroring what you did on the other side of the XL-Motor with another Cross Axle Extension. The 2M Axle goes in the Zero Degree Element.

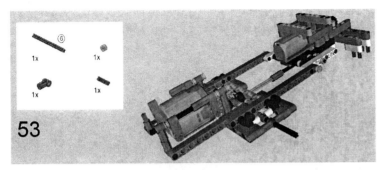

Figure 5-103. As you can see, the 6M Axle joins up with the XL-Motor and will help hold it in place.

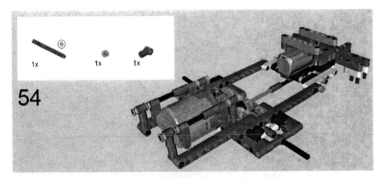

Figure 5-104. At this point, the XL-Motor should be completely secured.

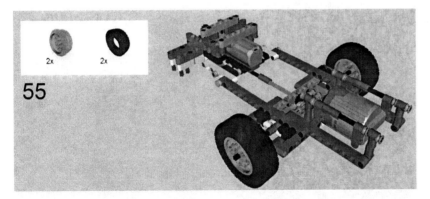

Figure 5-105. Time to add on the wheels, at least on the back. These are 56 x 28 tires, but you can use bigger ones or ones with more traction if you can make them fit.

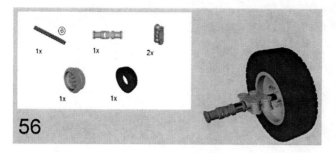

Figure 5-106. Prepare the first front tire, which needs a secure axle, with the two Double Cross Blocks and a Universal Joint. Leave some room on the axle between the Cross Blocks and Tire Rim, as this will come into play later.

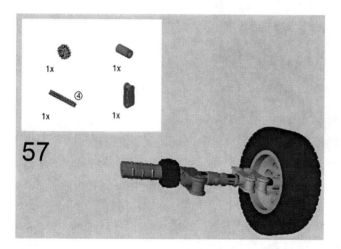

Figure 5-107. Add on a 4M Axle with a 3M Cross Block, Cross Axle Extension, and the Z12 Conical Wheel Gear.

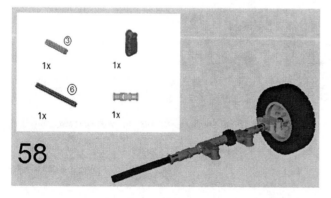

Figure 5-108. Again, add some essential parts to the axle: a 3M Axle, a 3M Cross Block, a Universal Joint, and a 6M Axle, in that order.

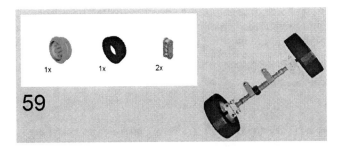

Figure 5-109. To complete this axle, add the other tire, leaving some room to spare between the Double Cross Blocks and Tire Rim.

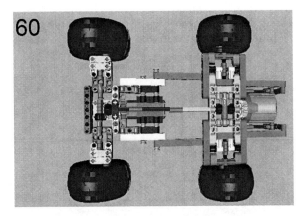

Figure 5-110. Now put the front axle on. Be certain that the gear meshes and is on the proper side and that all Connector Peg/Cross Axles fit in correctly.

░ **Note** Before beginning this project, refer to Appendix A for a complete list of required parts.

Reviewing the 4 X 4 Construction

If you built this vehicle correctly, with one flick of the propulsion controls all four wheels will turn in the same direction. You should be able to fit the IR-RX on it wherever you like, connect the engines, and run it around the room, taking control of the speed and the steering.

If you need to adjust the rack and pinion, you can take off the front-most gear and adjust it manually if necessary. The two levers applied in Step 44 (Figure 5-94) will be the catch that makes certain the gear does not spin too much. This should give you an idea of how to build a 4 x 4 vehicle that you can modify for you own creations; you can attach whatever tires will give you the most traction. If you like, you can combine the shock absorbent back, the flexible front steering mechanism, and figure out how to work them together so you have a shock-absorbing 4 x 4 vehicle. Not to sound like too much of a tease, but I purposely did not include a grand set of instructions for this. I leave it to you as a challenge, if you are up to it.

You can also create a four-wheel drive vehicle with a double engine. All you need to do is hook up a motor in the left size to the tires on the left side, and then hook up a motor in the right side to the right side tires. The only way to do this is to create some combination of meshing gears and such, but I have already shown you ways of doing it.

Summary

LEGO Technic vehicles can be built to be very robust. They can be built so strong that they can even be made to be all-terrain, which works well if you are going to use remote control.

For example, the shock absorbing pieces create flexibility for the wheels of your vehicles. Also helpful are track rods, steering arms, and other pieces designed for such purposes. Some vehicles require extra thick tires with good treads, but sometimes, more is needed.

In addition to creating vehicles with more shock absorption, you should also consider making a 4 x 4, with all wheels in motion. The most difficult part is creating the steering mechanism for this, but the universal joint pieces are able to bring them all together into one axis for the motor.

■ ■ ■

CHAPTER 6

Technic Construction Vehicles and Equipment

The last few chapters focused on creating ordinary vehicles like cars that you can drive and steer by remote control. That might be enough for some of you LEGO Technic builders, but if you are going to build vehicles out of LEGO Technic pieces, then you might as well build some unusual vehicles. I am talking about the vehicles that can be found at construction sites, such as bulldozers, forklifts, dump trucks, and all manner of specialty-use equipment. LEGO has always been in the business of making vehicles that people want to build, and their earliest sets were of construction vehicles. It is no wonder that their first Technic sets were construction-themed with a bulldozer (Set 951) and a forklift (Set 950). Clearly, the company knew that builders wanted to create vehicles with some very unusual features.

For the most part thus far I have shown how to build complete models of vehicles, such as the 4 x 4 vehicle in Chapter 5. In this chapter, I am going to focus on specific portions of the featured models (truck hoe, bulldozer, forklift, and crane). For example, I will show you how to build a bulldozer swivel and scoop, but you will have to figure out how to build the bulldozer frame (with wheels) yourself. Other model sections that will be discussed are the lifting part of a forklift and the lifting section of a crane.

With these sections as your foundation, you can then decide how best to construct an entire model. As I said earlier in the book, I won't do all the creating for you; it wouldn't be very much fun for you if I did!

LEGO Technic Excavation

In my opinion, some of the coolest things at construction sites are the big excavators, such as track hoes, backhoes, and bulldozers. I'm not certain how dirty you want to get your particular LEGO Technic creations, but the project that follows shows you how to make some basic working construction features including a track hoe swivel and scoop plus a bulldozer blade, which are good for playing in the sand.

Project 6-1: Creating a Track Hoe Swivel

■ **Note**   Before beginning any projects in this chapter, refer to Appendix A for a complete list of required parts.

One of the advantages of a track hoe is that the driver can swivel around 180 degrees to scoop in any direction within reach. If you want something that can pivot in such a fashion, you can do so remotely or manually.

As you can see in Figure 6-1, LEGO has many types of swivel bricks known as "turntables" or "turning elements" that allow you manually spin your creation. These pieces come in handy for all kinds of spinning creations. In this project, I will show you how to use the turntable all the way to the right.

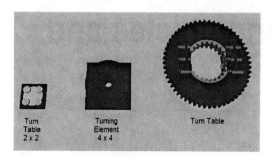

Figure 6-1. *LEGO Turntable pieces allow for 360 degree spinning on studded and studless creations.*

With the proper application of a smaller gear and a motor, you can also use a remote control to automatically spin the part. This alternative uses the Turntable piece with teeth around it, like a large gear as seen in Figure 6-1. If you want to set up a track hoe or crane with this swivel, follow the instructions in Figures 6-2 through 6-17.

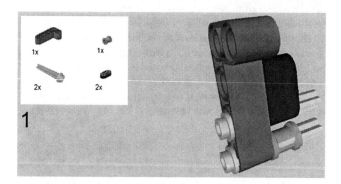

Figure 6-2. *Start with a 4 x 2 Angular Beam and then use two 3M Axles with stud as shown. Secure one Axle with two 2M Levers, and a Bush on the other.*

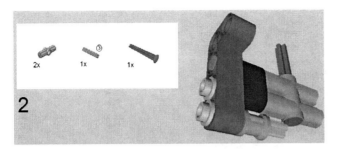

Figure 6-3. Connect a 180 Degree Element to the 3M Axle with Stud, and then connect a plain 3M Axle to the other 180 Degree Element. Connect the two 180 Degree Elements with the 4M Axle with Stop.

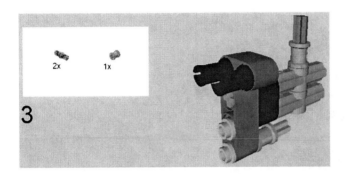

Figure 6-4. Put a Bush on the 4M Axle with Stop as shown, and add two Connector Pegs.

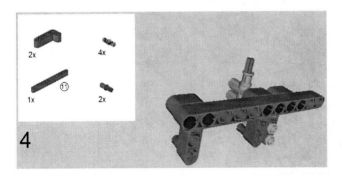

Figure 6-5. Take two 4 x 2 Angular Beams and add a Connector Peg/Cross Axlë to the Cross-Hole as shown. The four Connector Pegs link to the 4 x 2 Angular Beam, and a 11M Beam links them all together.

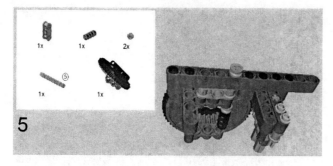

Figure 6-6. *The Turntable joins with the structure thanks to a 5M Axle, two Half-Bushes, a Double Cross Block, and a Cross Axle Extension.*

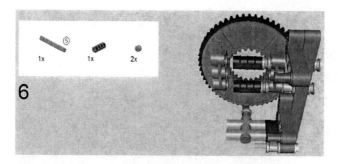

Figure 6-7. *I changed the view so you can see how the Turntable is doubly secured using another 5M Axle, Cross Axle Extension, and two Half-Bushes with the Double Cross Block.*

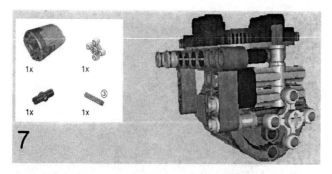

Figure 6-8. *Add the XL-Motor on the two Connector Peg/Cross Axles. Insert the 180 Degree Element on the 3M Axle with Stud, then place the 3M Axle into the XL-Motor. Add the Angular Gear" until flush.*

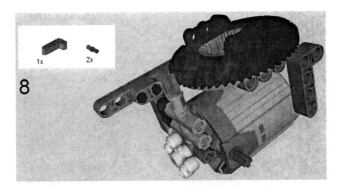

Figure 6-9. Turn the structure to the side and insert the Connector Peg/Cross Axles, like those on the other side, and then insert the 4 x 2 Angular Beam.

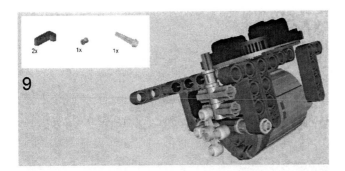

Figure 6-10. *Add two 4 x 2 Angular Beams as shown. The 3M with Stud and Bush help secure the 180 Degree Element on the bottom.*

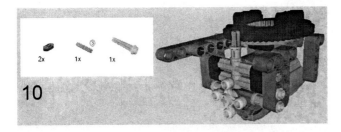

Figure 6-11. *Insert two 2M Levers and secure them with a 3M Axle and a 3M Axle with a Stud.*

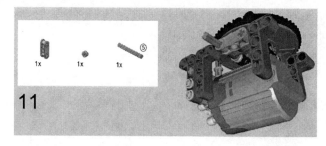

Figure 6-12. Insert a Half-Bush between the Turntable and the other end of the Cross Axle Extension, and join it with a 5M Axle. Then insert a Double Cross Block as shown.

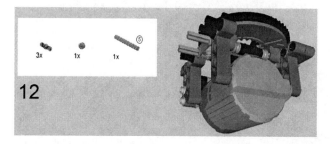

Figure 6-13. Add another 5M Axle and Half-Bush to join the Double Cross Block and Turntable. Three Connector Pegs go in as shown.

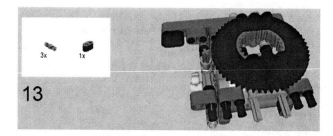

Figure 6-14. Add two more Connector Pegs to the side of the construction as shown, and use a Connector Peg to link the Cross and Hole piece to the other side.

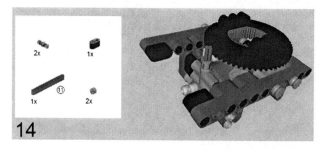

Figure 6-15. Add another two Connector Pegs on the one side, and then a 11M Beam. Insert the Cross and Hole Beam as well as the two Half-Bushes.

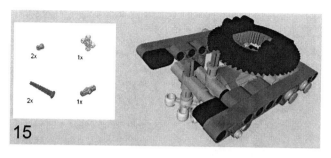

Figure 6-16. Insert the 4M Axle with Stop through the Cross and Hole Beam and join it with a Bush and 180 Degree Angle Element. Then insert another 4M Axle with Stop from below with another Bush and the Angular Gear.

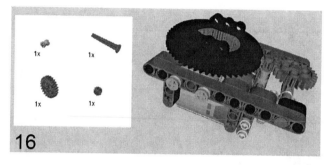

Figure 6-17. Another 4M with Stop and Bush join with the 180 Degree Angle Element in front of the construction. Now that this is secured in place, put the Gears on it as shown, and be sure they mesh together.

Once you are finished with Project 6-1, connect the battery box to the XL-Motor and make certain that the turntable spins freely. All you need to do now is decide what to put on your turntable/swivel; the six Connector Peg holes on top should be more than enough to create something incredible. Mounting this on your model with the motor could be a complex affair, depending on what type of model you are building. You may also want to attach the motor to the IR-RX discussed in previous chapters so you can control it remotely. The best part about putting a motor on this is that you don't have to worry about creating some sort of catch so the gears don't jam. In fact, you could make this swivel spin until the battery runs out.

If you are thinking about creating a scoop for a track hoe for this swivel, the instructions in Project 6-2 will help you do so.

Project 6-2: Creating a Scoop for a Bulldozer

A lot of the Technic bulldozer sets that I have seen use essentially the same principles of operation, and the setup can be quite complex. A simpler construction is the two-lever scoop found in many playground sandboxes, such as the one in Figure 6-18. The construction is simple: one lever adjusts the scoop at a pivoting angle and the other lever raises the scoop itself.

Figure 6-18. *A sandbox scoop on a playground—a great unit to model in Technic pieces.*

The instructions in Figures 6-19 through 6-33 show you how to create the scoop in Figure 6-18 with Technic LEGO pieces.

■ **Note** The scoop is not very long in comparison to the shovel on the end. I recommend making the scoop a lot bigger.

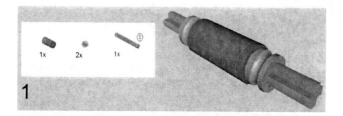

Figure 6-19. *Begin with a 5M Axle, a Tube, and two Half Bushes.*

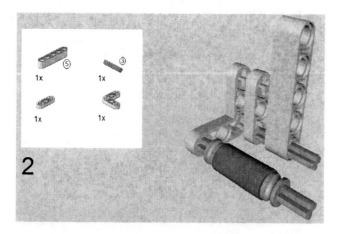

Figure 6-20. *Add a 3M Axle to a 5M Beam, and then add it to a 3M Lever. Add a 3 x 3 90 Degree Lever to the 5M Axle. You will have two separate constructions, but they will be assembled in the next step.*

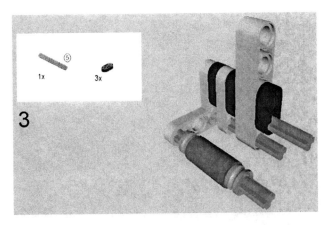

Figure 6-21. Attach three 2M Levers to another 5M Axle and then join the 5M Beam.

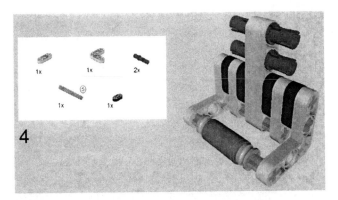

Figure 6-22. To complete the end of the scoop, add another 5M Axle to an additional 2M Lever, 3M Lever, and 3 x 3 90 Degree Lever. Add two 3M Connector Pegs to the 5M Beam.

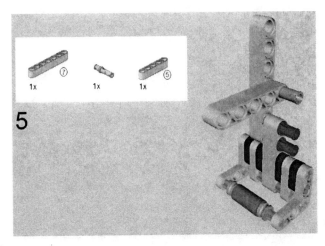

Figure 6-23. Add another 5M Beam via a 3M Connector Peg without Friction.

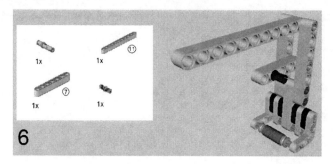

Figure 6-24. Attach a 11M Beam to the 7M Beam with a 3M Connector Peg without Friction. Attach a 7M Beam to one side and a Connector Peg to the 5M Beam.

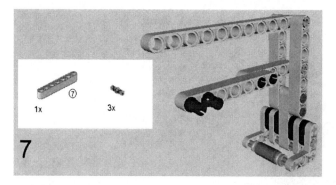

Figure 6-25. Add a Connector Peg to the 5M Beam, and then add a 7M Beam on those. Place two Connector Pegs on the 7M Beam.

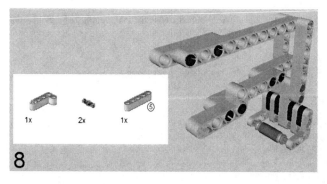

Figure 6-26. Add a 4 x 2 Beam to the 7M Beam from the previous step. Add a 5M Beam to the 11M Beam with Connector Pegs.

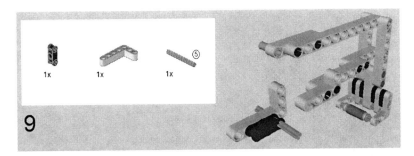

Figure 6-27. This separate part of the structure consists of a Double Cross Block, a 5M Axle, and a 5 x 3 Angular Beam.

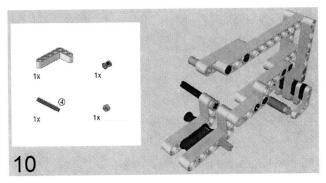

Figure 6-28. Add another 5 x 3 Angular Beam with a Bush on the 5M Axle. Place a 4M Axle with a Half Bush on top.

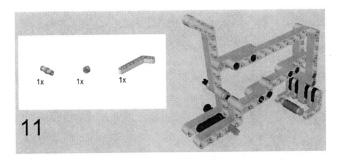

Figure 6-29. Line up the rest of the Scoop with the construction made in the last two steps and add a Connector Peg with a 3 x 7 Technic Beam.

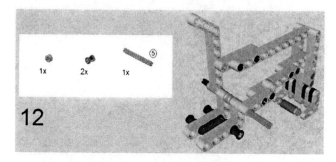

Figure 6-30. Join a 5M Axle via a Half Bush. Add the Bushes on the construction as shown.

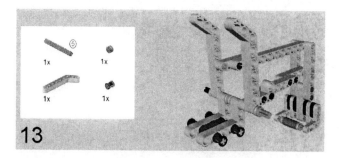

Figure 6-31. Add a 5M Axle with a Bush. Insert a 3 x 7 Technic Beam with the Half-Bush.

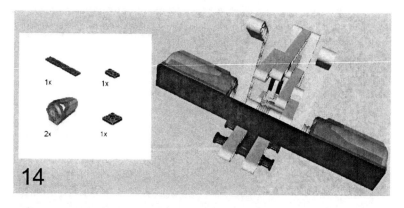

Figure 6-32. Insert two M-Motors to the Axles as shown, and then connect a 2 x 12 Plate to join them together. Use the 1 x 2 Plate and 2 x 2 Plate to fill in the two together.

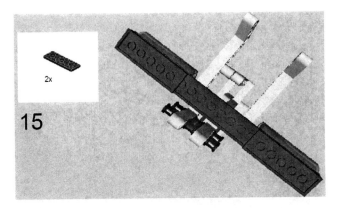

Figure 6-33. *The last step involves adding on 2 x 6 Plates to secure the M-Motors in place.*

As you can see in Figure 6-33, you can connect two M-Motors to each side of the 3 x 7 Angular Beams and link them together with a long LEGO Plate. You can then hook these up to the IR-RX to take control of them. I found that with a model of this size, the speed of the motors worked against me, so you might want to put some gears in to slow things down a bit. Also, the longer the scoop, the slower it will rise.

To secure the scoop to the swivel, just remove the bushes from Steps 10, 13, and 14 and insert the scoop into the swivel as shown in Figure 6-34.

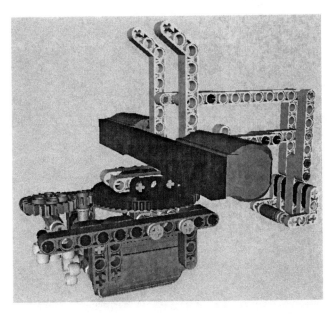

Figure 6-34. *It is quite simple to attach the swivel to the scoop.*

Project 6-3: Building a Rack and Pinion Forklift

If you ever worked in a warehouse, then you know the importance of a forklift. There are several ways of building a forklift in LEGO Technic, depending on which pieces you have. In this project, I use the rack and pinion method discussed in Chapter 3; this will raise the forks and allows them to stay up, thanks to the power of gears.

This project sets up a forklift in two parts. The first part is the rack portion with the toothed racks (Steps 1-8 in Figures 6-35 through 6-42), followed by the pinion portion with a toothed gear (Steps 9-25 in Figures 6-43 through 6-59).

Creating the Rack Portion of the Forklift

Follow Steps 1-8 in Figures 6-35 through 6-42 to make the rack portion of the forklift.

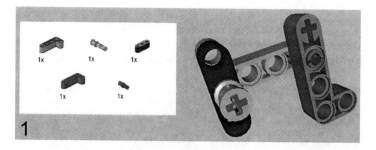

Figure 6-35. *Start with two 4 x 2 Angular Beams and a 3M Beam. Use a Snap with Friction and a Connector Peg/Cross Axle to join them together.*

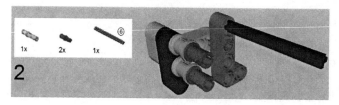

Figure 6-36. *Join a 6M Axle to the 4 x 2 Beam. Add a Friction Snap and then two Connector Peg/Cross Axles.*

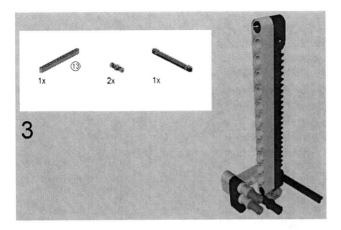

***Figure 6-37.** Join a 13M Rack with a 3M Beam via two Connector Pegs, and then join them up with the 6M Axle.*

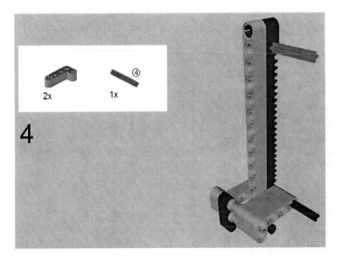

***Figure 6-38.** Attach two 4 x 2 Beams on the 6M Axle, and insert the 4M Axle into the 3M Rack.*

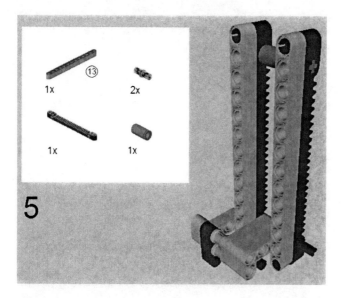

Figure 6-39. *Note the tube at the top, inserted before the Rack and 13M Beam. Attach a 13M Beam to a 13M Rack and put it on the axles.*

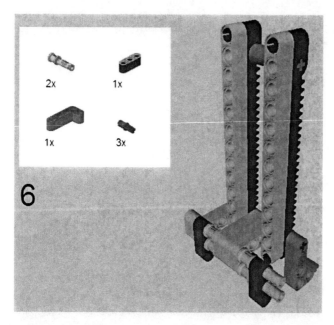

Figure 6-40. *Place a Connector Peg/Cross Axle to join with a 4 x 2 Angular Beam. Connect the remaining Connector Peg/Cross Axles to the Friction Snaps and join them with the 3M Beam as shown.*

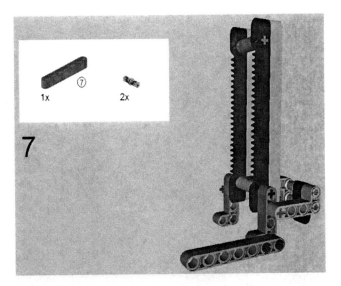

Figure 6-41. Attach two Connector Pegs to the 4 x 2 Angular Beam and then attach a 7M Beam.

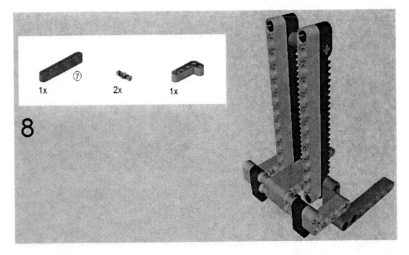

Figure 6-42. Add on a 4 x 2 Angular Beam, and then add on a 7M Beam to another 4 x2 Angular Beam with two Connector Pegs.

Creating the Pinion Portion of the Forklift

Follow the instructions in Figures 6-43 through 6-59 to complete the forklift.

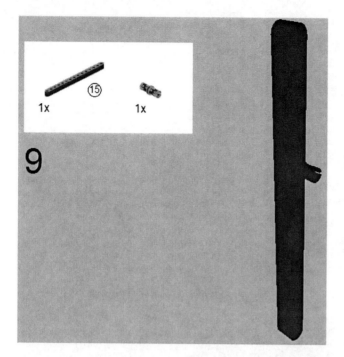

Figure 6-43. To start, add a Connector Peg with a 15M Beam.

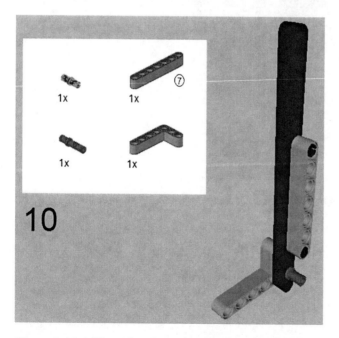

Figure 6-44. Add another Connector Peg on the 15M Beam, and then join it with a 7M Beam. Connect a 5 x 3 Angular Beam to the opposite side of the 15M Beam with the 3M Connector Peg.

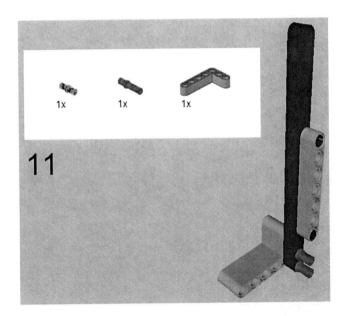

Figure 6-45. Link the 5 x 3 Angular Beam with the other one using the Connector Peg, then add the 3M Connector Peg on the opposite side.

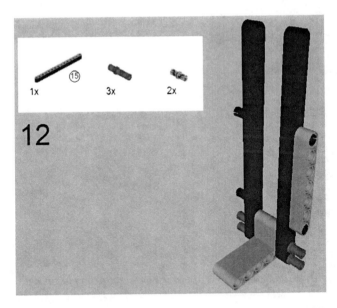

Figure 6-46. Use three 3M Connector Pegs, and join a 15M Beam on the same side. Attach two Connector Pegs as shown.

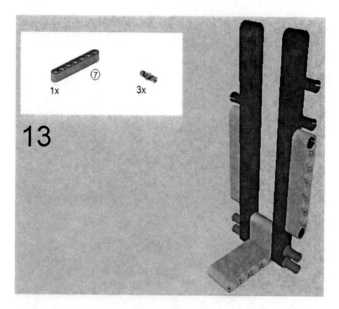

Figure 6-47. Another 7M Beam joins here, and three Connector Pegs join on each side of the 15M Beams.

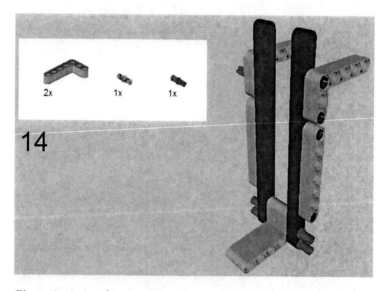

Figure 6-48. Another Connector Peg joins here, with an additional 5 x 3 Angular Beam. Note the placement of the Connector Peg/Cross Axle.

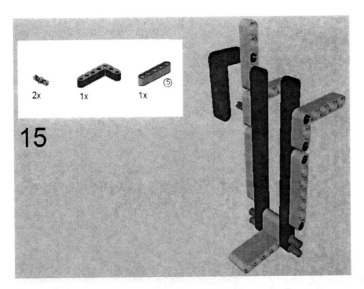

Figure 6-49. One Connector Peg goes atop the 15M Beam, and then a 5M Beam. Use a Connector Peg to place a 5 x 3 Angular Beam here. None of these parts will stand on their own, but they will be joined up later.

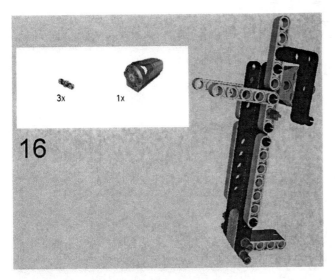

Figure 6-50. I changed the angle so that you can see where the Connector Pegs go on the M-Motor, as well as the Connector Peg goes on the 5 x 3 Angular Beam.

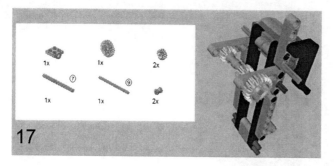

Figure 6-51. *A 2 x 2 Plate with Holes affixes to the M-Motor, and a 9M Axle secures it even more. The 7M Axle links with the two Double Bevel Gears (Z12) two Bushes, and the Z20 Double Bevel Gear.*

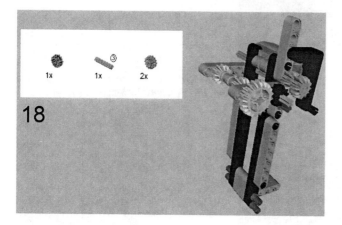

Figure 6-52. *Place two Double Bevel Gears (Z12) on the 9M Axle. Place the other Z12 Double Bevel Gear in the center of the 3M Axle, and insert it as shown.*

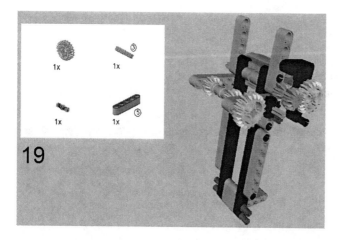

Figure 6-53. *The 3M Axle joins with the M-Motor and the Z20 Double Bevel Gear. Another 5M Beam joins the other side with the Connector Peg.*

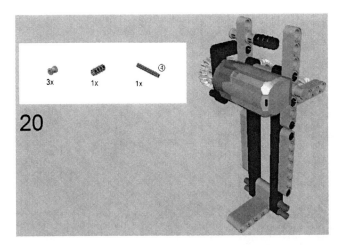

Figure 6-54. A Bush caps off the end of the 9M Axle. Add a 4M Axle on top, and then use two Bushes and the Cross-Axle Extension.

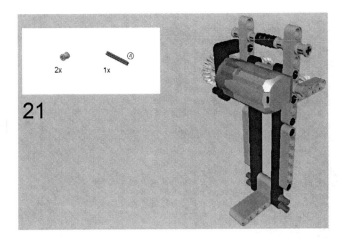

Figure 6-55. Add another 4M Axle, with two Bushes on top of the structure.

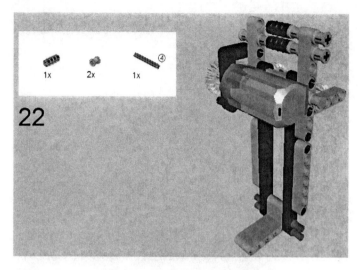

Figure 6-56. It is again time to place a 4M Axle with two Bushes atop the structure.

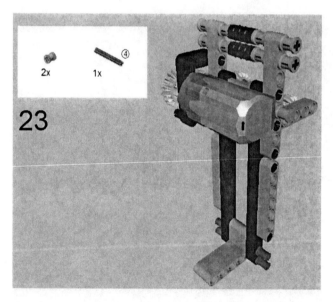

Figure 6-57. With the application of two Bushes and a 4M Axle, complete the top of the structure as shown.

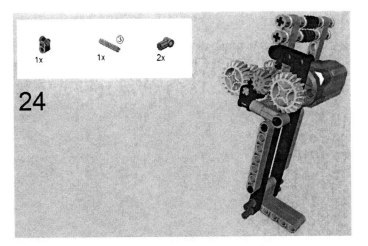

Figure 6-58. Connect the two Zero Degree Elements together with the 3M Axle and the 1 x 2 Cross Block. Insert it on the model as shown to lock the M-Motor securely to the structure.

This last step is going to be a little tricky, as it requires taking part of the secondary unit apart to do it. Just remove the Bushes from the two 6M Axles on top, and slide off the 5 x 3 Beams in between. Then place the first unit in so the gears mesh with the top of the racks, and put the 6M Bushes and Axles back in.

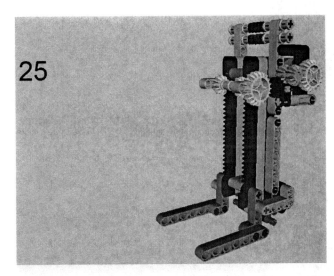

Figure 6-59. This is what your model will look like when you connect the rack section with the pinion section.

If you want to use a gear method, you could do so, but it might be pretty complicated as the motorized spinning would have to take place atop the forks and not at the bottom. Another method is to create a crane that will lift the forks, so let's discuss how to make a crane next.

Project 6-4: Building a Crane

Cranes require string, and it is pretty easy to put a motor on for extending and retracting. You might want to put an extender on the end, with the use of a rack and pinion mechanism, so follow the instructions in Figures 6-60 through 6-87.

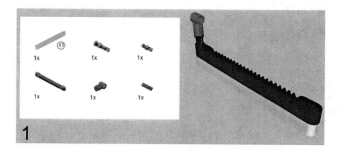

Figure 6-60. This is a separate construction from the crane, which will be joined in the last Step. Join the 13M Rack to the 13M Beam with a Connector Peg. Note the Zero Degree Element, 2M Axle, and Friction Snap.

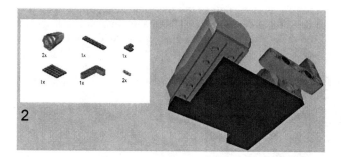

Figure 6-61. Take two M-Motors and attach the 2 x 6 Plate, 1 x 6 Plate, and 2 x 2 Edge Plate as shown. Attach the two Connector Pegs to one of the M-Motors and attach the 5 x 3 Angular Beams to it.

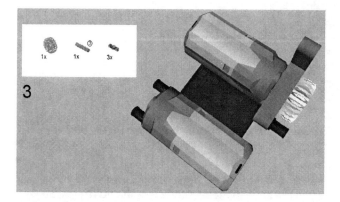

Figure 6-62. Attach two Connector Pegs on the other motor, and then attach another one on the 5 x 3 Angular Beam. Insert the 3M into the M-Motor and slide on a Z20 Double Bevel Gear.

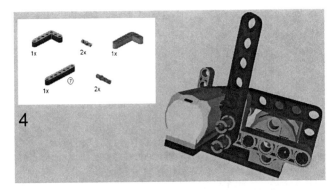

Figure 6-63. Note the placement of the two 5 x 3 Angular Beams, with the Connector Pegs. Attach the 7M Beam to this with the 3M Connector Pegs.

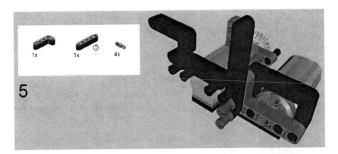

Figure 6-64. Connect four Connector Pegs to the 5M Beam as shown, and then connect a 4 x 2 Angular Beam to that. Line it up as shown, for it will be attached in the next step.

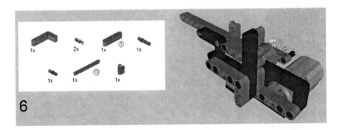

Figure 6-65. The 5 x 3 Beam connects the parts from the last step here. Attach the 5M Beam to the 7M Beam, and then connect the 13M Beam to that. Note the application of the Connector Peg/Cross Axle, and how the 3M Connector Peg attaches to the Cross Block.

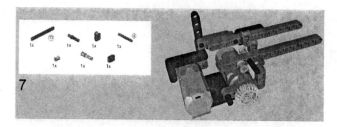

Figure 6-66. Switch over to the other side of the construction, and attach the parts to the 13M Beam as shown. Much of it looks similar to the other side, except for the Friction Snap connected to the Cross and Hole Beam as well as the 4M Axle with Bush.

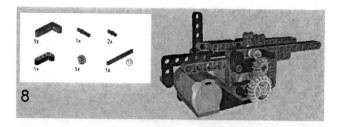

Figure 6-67. In this step, you need to insert a 3M Connector Peg through the corner hole of a 5 x 3 Angular Beam, then link it to the corner hole of a 4 x 2 Angular Beam. Put this in place, and then insert the Connector Peg/Cross Axle to the Z12 Double Bevel Angular Gear.

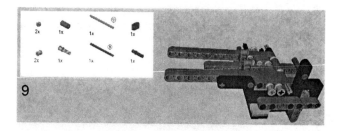

Figure 6-68. Switch to the other side of the creation. The Friction Snap and Cross and Hole Beam join here, and the 8M and 9M Axles help join these sides together. The Bushes, Half-Bushes, and Tube join them together.

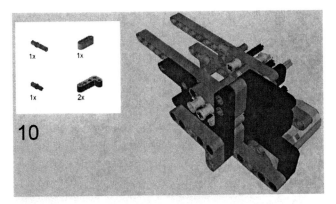

Figure 6-69. Another 3M Connector Peg joins the 7M Beam, and a 3M Beam joins the construction as shown. Two 4 x 2 Angular Beams join here, and one of them needs a Connector Peg/Cross Axle to attach properly.

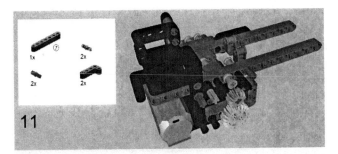

Figure 6-70. Another 7M Beam joins the construction on this other side, and lines up here with two 4 x 2 Angular Beams. Note the placement of the Connector Peg/Cross Axles and Connector Pegs.

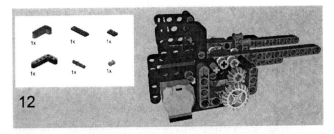

Figure 6-71. Apply the 1 x 4 and 1 x 2 Plates on the bottom of the M-Motor on this side to fill in the gaps below. Connect the 5 x 3 Beam to the 13M Beam with the 3M Connector, and attach the 4 x 2 Beam as shown. Don't forget to apply the Bush.

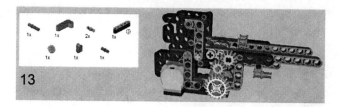

Figure 6-72. Attach the 5M Beam to the construction and attach a Z12 Gear so it meshes with the other one as shown. Attach the Cross Block and the 4 x 2 Angular Beam as well.

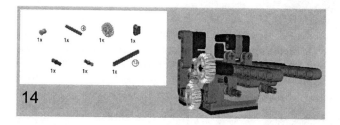

Figure 6-73. Add another 13M Beam, along with a Cross Block, Connector Peg, and Connector Peg/Cross Axle. Attach a 4M Axle to the Z20 Double Bevel Gear and Bush and make certain they mesh together.

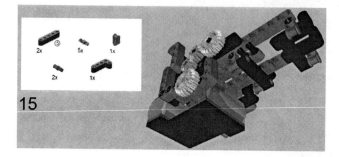

Figure 6-74. The 5M Beam connects to the Connector Peg/Cross Axles. Attach the rest of the pieces together and put it in front of the model. It will be connected in the next step.

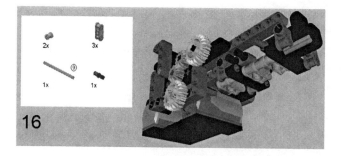

Figure 6-75. A 9M Axle goes between the two 5M Beams, and the Double Cross Blocks and Bushes secure it in place. Note the placement of the Connector Peg/Cross Axle.

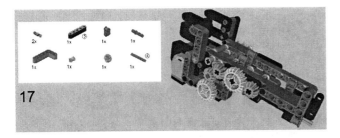

Figure 6-76. Most of these parts are on this side shown, like the Z12 Double Bevel Gear, 4M Axle, Bush, 3M Connector Peg, Cross Block, and 5 x 3 Angular Beam. The 5M Beam also goes here, but is not visible in this picture. If you can't see where to put it, make certain it mirrors the placement of the 5M in Step 18.

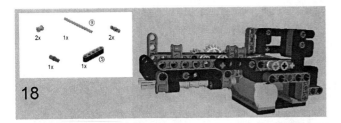

Figure 6-77. Add another 9M Axle and Bushes, and add a 5M Beam to the side as shown, secured with the Connector Pegs and Connector Peg/Cross Axle.

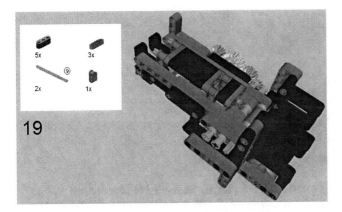

Figure 6-78. Focus goes to the top of the construction as 9M Axles secure three 3M Levers and five 3M Beams. The Cross Block helps secure it in place as well.

Figure 6-79. *Add another Z20 Double Bevel Gear, 4M Axle, and Bush to mesh with the other Double Bevel Gears on this side. On the opposite side, add the Connector Peg and 3M Connector Peg.*

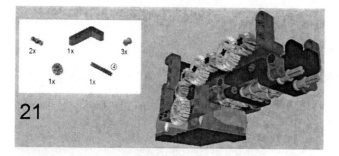

Figure 6-80. *Add another section with a Double Bevel Gear. Place two Bushes in front of it, and don't forget to add the 5 x 3 Angular Beam.*

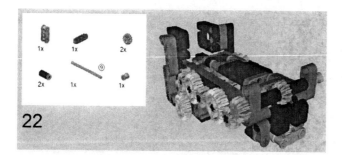

Figure 6-81. *The Double Cross Block goes in front, on the 9M Axles below. Slide the 3M Lever to cap off another set of 9M Axles above. Slide another 9M Axle with the Bush, Tubes, and Z12 Double Bevel Gears to create the section in front that you can see here.*

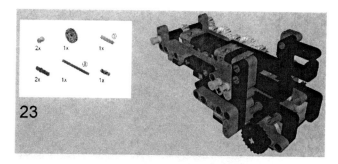

Figure 6-82. *The Z20 Double Bevel Gear and 3M Axle join with the M-Motor. Two 3M Connector Pegs join here, and the 8M Axle joins as shown, to be secured with a Bush in the center. Add another Bush as shown.*

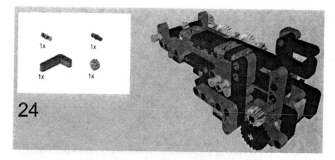

Figure 6-83. *The Connector Pegs and Connector Peg/Cross Axles join the 5 x 3 Angular Beam. Make certain that the Z12 Double Bevel Gear meshes with the other Z20 Double Bevel Gear.*

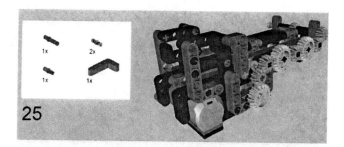

Figure 6-84. *The Connector Pegs of various sizes help the 5 x 3 Angular Beam join with the rest of the construction.*

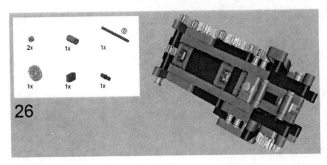

Figure 6-85. I shifted to a top view so you can see how the 8M Axle, Tube, Half-Bushes, Cross and Hole Beam, and Connector Peg/Cross Axle join here. You can see a better view in the next step—just make certain that the Z20 Double Bevel Beam meshes with the Gears below it.

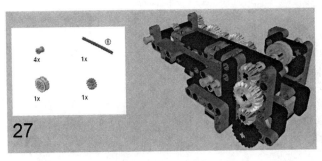

Figure 6-86. Slide an 8M Axle on top with the four Bushes, as well as whatever you will be using as a "spindle" for your crane string. Make certain that it meshes with the other gears.

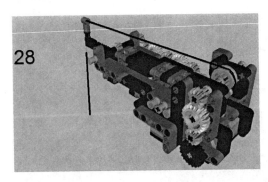

Figure 6-87. You might have to detach some of the parts in Step 22 to do this last step, but you will need to slide in the construction from Step 1 so it meshes with the Z12 Double Bevel Gear in the center of the construction. If you remove the 9M Axle, Tubes, and other parts in front, you should have no trouble placing it in.

As you can see in Figure 6-87, you have a way of putting some string through the spindle to simulate crane cable, and you can put any hook or even a wrecking ball on the other end. Want to reach higher heights? No problem! Just extend the rack that you installed in Step 28. Of course, it takes more than just an extension and cable to make a crane. What you need is a way of raising that hook high so you handle loads from above.

Project 6-5: Raising the Crane with a Worm Gear

This next construction can be used with Project 6-4, but it can be used with other construction equipment related projects such as a bulldozer front blade, dump truck, or any other project that requires a worm gear to get it to work.

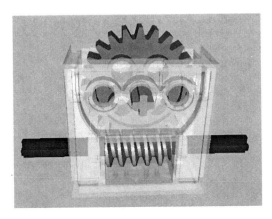

Figure 6-88. This is the setup for a Worm Gear meshed with a Z24 Gear Wheel.

You can see in Figure 6-88 the setup of a Worm Gear, which is the screw-shaped piece mounted horizontally. If you turn the Worm Gear, this will spin the Z24 Gear Wheel. Attaching something secure to the gear wheel, such as an axle, will insure that it will rise. Attaching a motor to the Worm Gear Axle will help the rotating/raising motion, but you should note that spinning the Z24 Gear Wheel will not spin the Worm Gear. Figures 6-89 through 6-107 show you the steps.

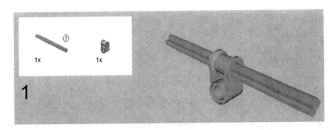

Figure 6-89. Take a Technic 1 x 2 Cross Block and center it on a 7M Axle.

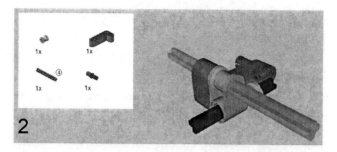

Figure 6-90. Slide a 4 x 2 Angular Beam and attach it to a Connector Peg/Cross Axle. Slide a 4M Cross Axle with a Bush on it so there is 1M of Axle on each side.

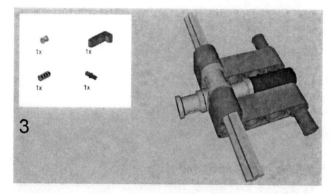

Figure 6-91. I shifted the angle so you can see where to put the next 4 x 2 Angular Beam and the Connector Peg/Cross Axle. Connect the Bush and Cross Axle Extension on the 4M Axle.

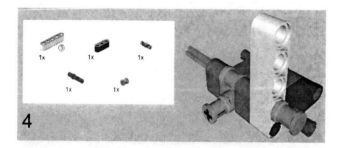

Figure 6-92. Add on a 5M Beam with a Connector Peg and secure it with a Bush. Place a 3M Beam on the same side and secure it with a 3M Connector Peg.

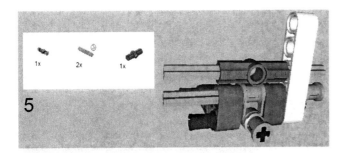

Figure 6-93. Take a 180 Degree Angle Element and put the 3M Axles on each side. Slide it into the 5M Beam as shown, and attach the Connector Peg to the 4 x 2 Angular Beam.

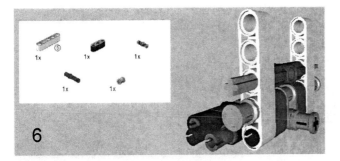

Figure 6-94. Slide another 5M beam along with a Bush so it matches the other side. Use the 3M Beam and 3M Connector Peg to also match the other side, then add the Connector Peg.

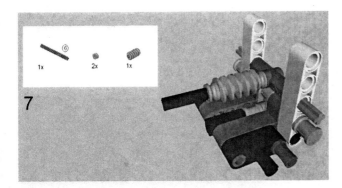

Figure 6-95. Slide a 6M Axle with two Half-Bushes and a Worm Gear. There should be 2M of bare Axle like you see here.

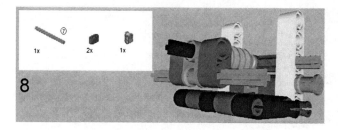

Figure 6-96. *Take a 7M Axle and slide on two Cross and Hole Beams and a 1 x 2 Cross Block. Slide that onto the 6M Axle from Step 7.*

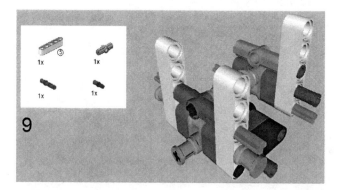

Figure 6-97. *Attach a 3M Connector Peg to a 5M Beam. Connect the 180 Degree Element to the 5M Beam via Connector Peg/Cross Axle. Slide the section on the 7M Axle from Step 8.*

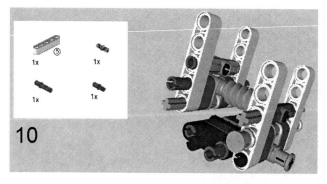

Figure 6-98. *Attach a Connector Peg/Cross Axle with a 3M Connector Peg to a 5M Axle. Slide it so it matches the other side, and place a Connector Peg in the center of the 180 Degree Element.*

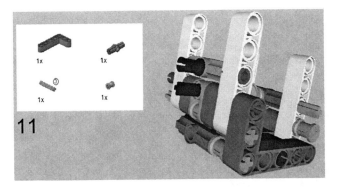

Figure 6-99. Place the 5 x 3 Angular Beam on it to lock two sides of the structure together. Connect a 180 Degree Element with a Bush and 3M Axle, and slide it into place.

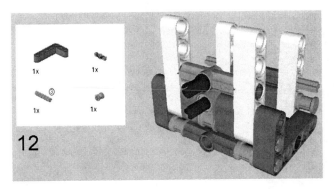

Figure 6-100. Add a Bush plus a 3M Axle. Place a Connector Peg on the 3M Beam, and then place the 5 x 3 Beam to lock it all into place.

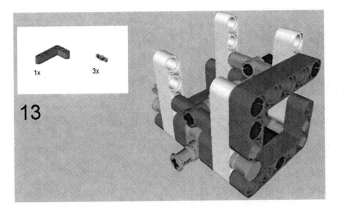

Figure 6-101. Use three Connector Pegs to lock another 5 x 3 Angular Beam into place.

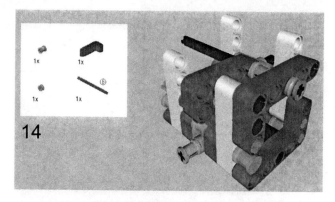

Figure 6-102. *Slide an 8M Axle as shown, along with the Bush, the 4 x 2 Angular Beam, and a Half-Bush.*

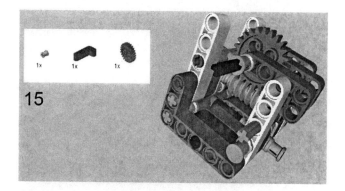

Figure 6-103. *Slide a 24 Tooth Gear on the 8M Axle so it meshes with the Worm Gear below, then slide on another 4 x 2 Angular Beam and Bush.*

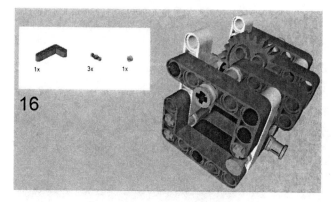

Figure 6-104. *Three Connector Pegs allow the 5 x 3 Angular Beam to lock into place, and the Half-Bush locks into place.*

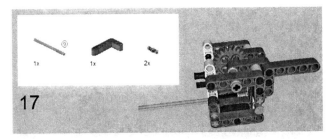

Figure 6-105. Two Connector Pegs lock a 5 x 3 Angular Beam with a 4 x 2 Angular Beam. Connect the 9M Axle to a Cross Axle Extension.

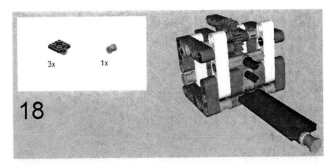

Figure 6-106. Slide three 2 x 2 Plates with Holes, and place a Bush to secure them into place.

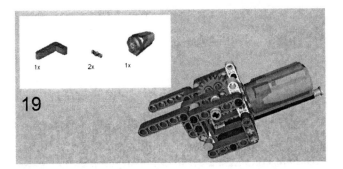

Figure 6-107. Use two more Connector Pegs to secure another 5 x 3 Angular Beam to a 4 x 2 Beam. The M-Motor, which provides power for the lift, fits on the 2 x 2 Plates and in front as well.

If you take off the two 5 x 3 Angular Beams in front of Project 6-5, you will find that it is quite easy to mount Project 6-4 there. Figure 6-108 shows how it looks.

Figure 6-108. *It is quite easy to mount Project 6-4 to Project 6-5 to make a crane that will raise up.*

By the way, if you want to connect both Project 6-4 and Project 6-5 to Project 6-1, you can (see Figure 6-109). All that is required is take out two 3M Beams at the bottom of Project 6-5, and you shouldn't have too much difficulty attaching it.

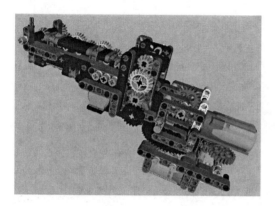

Figure 6-109. *When Project 6-1, 6-4, and 6-5 attach together, you have a recipe for a crane that can raise, swivel, and extend.*

Summary

Building construction equipment and vehicles from Technic LEGO pieces has been a staple since LEGO Technic's conception. Considering all the things that LEGO Technic allows, it is no surprise. For example, if you want to build a bulldozer or track hoe, it is very easy to also make a swivel with a working motor. It is also simple to make a scoop, and the one that I provided is based on the scoops in playground sandboxes.

For the forklift, a rack and pinion method can make for all sorts of interesting lifting. The Rack and Pinion method is also helpful for cranes, which can also be automated with a motor and a spindle of string.

It is also easy to build a method of raising the crane to bring the load on the hook up high. This type of model can be built with the help of a worm gear and can be rebuilt into a dump truck or some other type of vehicle with a ramp of some kind.

In short, I have given you what you need in this chapter to be constructive (pun intended).

CHAPTER 7

■ ■ ■

LEGO Technic Aviation: Airplanes and Helicopters

The Technic LEGO system has a few airplane kits, and although none of them have actually flown through the air (as of yet), they are of pretty good quality. Not only do they allow a user to create a miniature replica of some of their favorite aircraft, but they often have some features that make them very realistic.

This chapter will cover how to construct a basic LEGO Technic airplane and how to "give it wings." I assume that if you are going to build an airplane, then you want it to have the attributes and abilities of real airplanes like working propellers, flaps, and a rudder.

I will start with the basic part of a plane: the fuselage. This is the main body of the plane, and I will show you how to look at a plane and figure out how to "think in LEGO" so you can create it with LEGO Technic bricks. I won't discuss jet aircraft in detail, but I will discuss how to create a single-propeller plane and how to add as many propellers as you want on the wings. I'll also show you how to make some landing gear that you can retract, plus other necessities of a plane like flaps and a rudder. Finally, I'll also show you how to make the LEGO Technic helicopter—one with a spinning top rotor and side rotor!

Let's get down to business. I'll start by discussing how to create a flying machine (or a replica of an airplane) with some Technic bricks.

Choosing an Airplane to Model

In Chapter 2, I discussed the concept of wireframing and how to create a LEGO vehicle like a car by drawing a side view and then building around it. In the same manner, the basic form of an airplane (also known as the fuselage) can be formed. Like the LEGO Technic Smart Car in Chapter 2, you can add ideas of what you would like on it. I recommend looking at pictures of planes for inspiration.

For example, Figure 7-1 is a plane known as the Avro Andover, a 1920s British military transport aircraft originally constructed by a company known as Avro for the Royal Air Force (RAF). Avro made four different types of aircraft known as the 561, which is a flying ambulance.

Figure 7-1. The Avro Andover, a British military plane from the 1920s.

The Avro Andover has some interesting curves, but I found that its basic structure was like that of a capsule pill, so I drew a wireframe that resembles the fuselage of the aircraft (Figure 7-2).

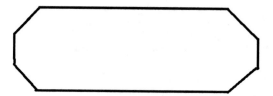

Figure 7-2. A very crude wireframe model of the Avro Andover plane, so I can build it in LEGO Technic bricks.

Project 7-1: Creating a Single Propeller Engine

Now that you've got a wireframe model, you can construct it. In the case of the Avro Andover, this isn't very difficult. The best part of a single propeller plane is that you can use LEGO Power Functions to put a propeller in front with one of the motors. You will find that a frame for a plane with a single propeller requires nothing more than a single XL-Motor and battery box (8881) to get the rotors spinning.

The steps shown in Figures 7-3 through 7-40 explain the fuselage (the part that carries the payload, minus the wings, tail, or other airplane parts).

■ **Note**   Before beginning any projects in this chapter, refer to Appendix A for a complete list of required parts.

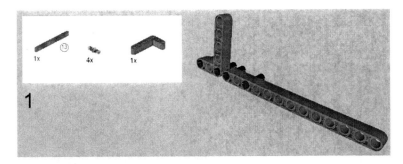

Figure 7-3. Start with a 13M Beam beside a 5 x 3 Angular Beam with four Connector Pegs.

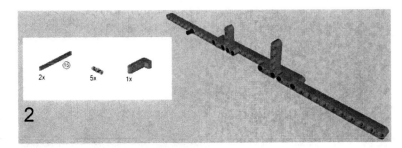

Figure 7-4. Join together two 15M Beams with the Connector Pegs and the 4 x 2 Angular Beam.

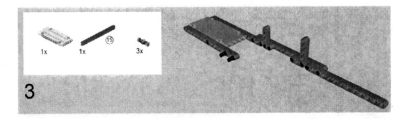

Figure 7-5. Attach the Flat Panel with a Connector Peg, like on its other side. The 15M Beam connects here as well.

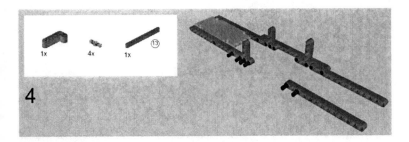

Figure 7-6. Set up a 4 x 2 Angular Beam and a 13M Beam as shown here, each with two Connector Pegs.

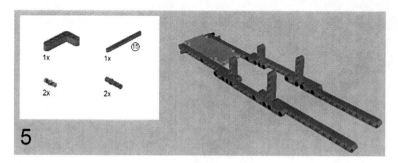

Figure 7-7. Note the placement of the 3M Connector Pegs as well as the 15M Beam along with the 5 x 3 Angular Beam. It should lock solidly together.

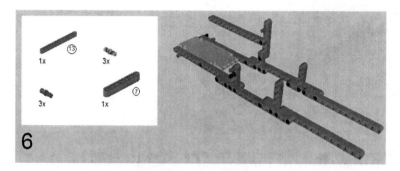

Figure 7-8. Note the additions to the 13M and 7M Beams here—the 7M Beam vertically and the 13M Beam horizontally. The 13M Beam will not stay horizontal when you use real LEGO Technic pieces due to gravity. Since this diagram was created with a 3D digital program, I didn't have to worry about real-life situations like gravity.

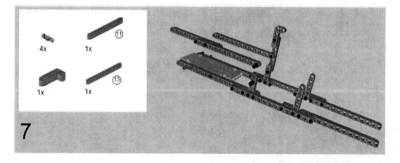

Figure 7-9. Attach a 4 x 2 Angular Beam on the 7M Beam. Attach the 13M and 11M Beams together here. Note that the 11M and 13M Beams are floating in air. Like the last step, it was created in a 3D program where gravity is not required. This will show you where the pieces will go when they are locked in place in the next step.

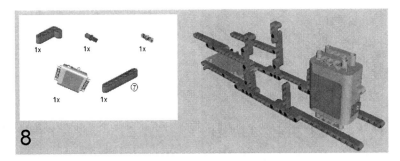

Figure 7-10. Place a 7M Beam and a 4 x 2 Angular Beam on the structure. The battery box also goes here, and it will be secured in the next step. The other Bush goes on the other side as a mirror image.

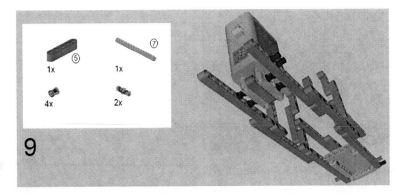

Figure 7-11. Place four Bushes in between the Battery box and Beams. The 5M Beam goes underneath and in between the two beam sections on the battery box. The two 7M Axles bring it all together. Note the placement of the two Connector Pegs.

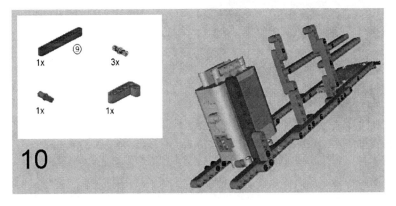

Figure 7-12. Join a 9M Beam and a 4 x 2 Angular Beam to the structure.

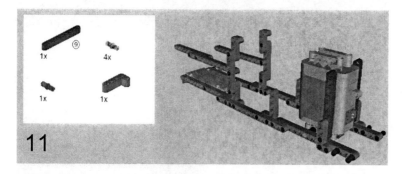

Figure 7-13. Join another side section to the structure on the other side, just like in Step 10.

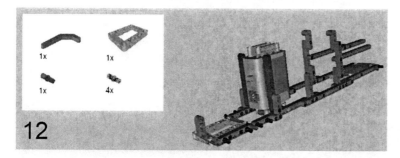

Figure 7-14. Add a 5 x 7 Beam Frame here with a Double Angular Beam.

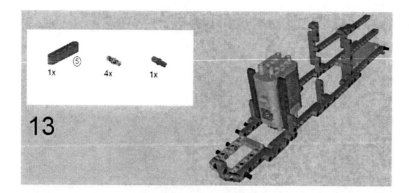

Figure 7-15. Attach a 5M Beam to the Double Angular Beam and the Connector Pegs to the 5 x 7 Beam Frame.

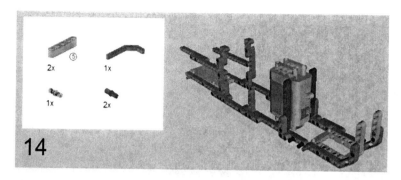

Figure 7-16. *Attach a Double Angle Beam and two 5M Beams with the Connector Pegs and Connector Peg/ Cross Axles.*

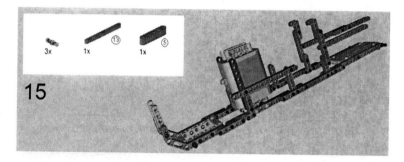

Figure 7-17. *Link a 13M Beam in the back of the battery box, horizontally. Note the application of a 5M Beam in front of the battery box.*

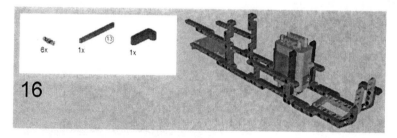

Figure 7-18. *Attach a 13M Beam to the structure horizontally via six Connector Pegs. Add the 4 x 2 Angular Beam in the front as shown.*

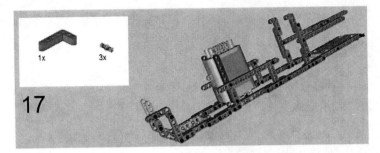

Figure 7-19. Now link the 5 x 3 Angular Beam to the front of the structure as shown.

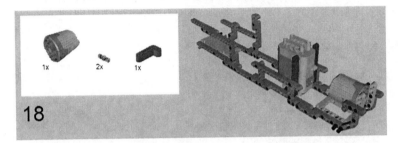

Figure 7-20. Add the XL-Motor to the 4 x 2 Beam in the front of the structure, and add another 4 x 2 Beam.

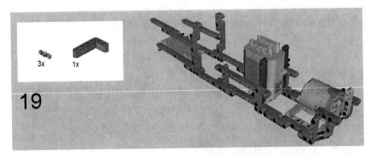

Figure 7-21. Add another 5 x 3 Angular Beam to help secure the XL-Motor into place.

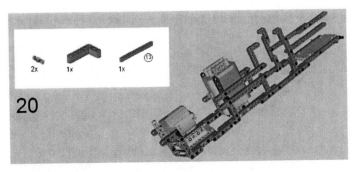

Figure 7-22. Add a 13M Beam as well as a 5 x 3 Beam on the side of the construction as shown.

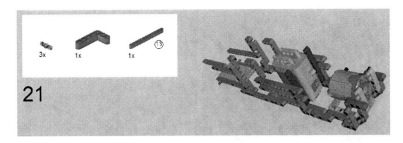

Figure 7-23. On the other side of the structure, join another 5 x 3 Angular Beam and 13M Beam.

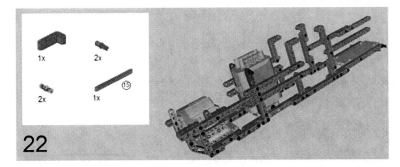

Figure 7-24. Add another 4 x 2 Beam to the XL-Motor with the Connector Peg and Connector Peg/Cross Axles, and then add a 15M Beam for more support.

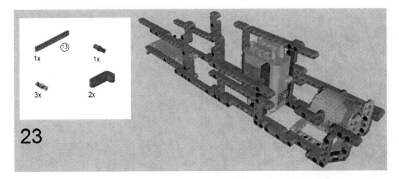

Figure 7-25. Join a 13M Beam with a 4 x 2 Beam, and attach this to the 9M beam on the right side of the construction. On the left side, add another 4 x 2 Beam to the XL-Motor.

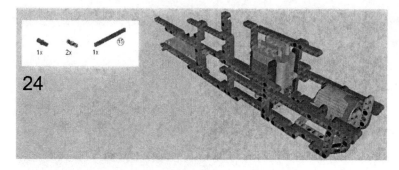

Figure 7-26. *Like the other side, a 15M Beam joins the two 4 x 2 Angular Beams attached to the XL-Motor.*

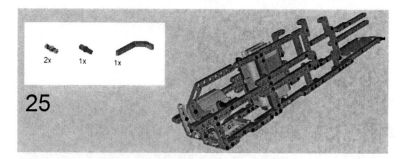

Figure 7-27. *A Connector Peg is placed on one of the 4 x 2 Angular Beam on the right side of the construction, and the Double Angular Beam joins with a vertical 5M Beam on the same side.*

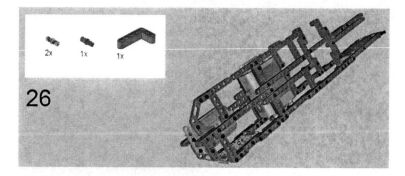

Figure 7-28. *A 5 x 3 Angular Beam joins up with the Double Angular Beam in front of the construction.*

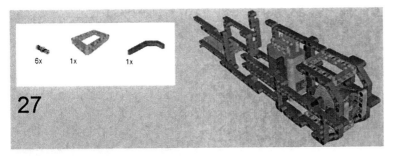

Figure 7-29. Another 5 x 7 Beam Frame joins with the front of the structure, as well as a Double Angular Beam.

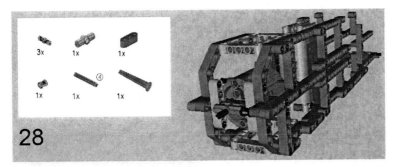

Figure 7-30. Take the 3M Beam and put Connector Pegs in its outermost holes (leave the center hole empty). Connect the 3M Beam to the XL-Motor, and then put in the 4M Axle. Place the 180 Degree Element over the Axle, and then use the 4M Axle with Stop to keep the 180 Degree Element in place.

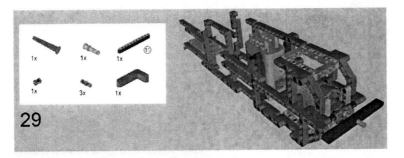

Figure 7-31. Go ahead and insert the 4M Axle with Stop, as you did on the opposite side in the previous step. Add the Friction Snap on the end of the central 4M Axle, and put the 11M Beam on it as shown for a propeller. Add the 5 x 3 Beam on the left side for more support.

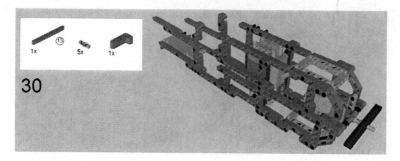

Figure 7-32. Attach a 4 x 2 Angular Beam to the 13M Beam, and then attach it to the left side of the structure.

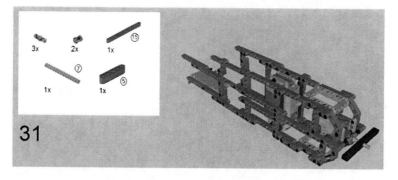

Figure 7-33. Add a 5M Beam to the battery box and use a 7M Axle and two Bushes to secure it to the structure. Note the application of the 15M Beam behind the battery box.

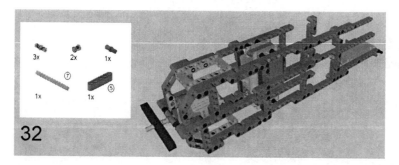

Figure 7-34. Use the two Bushes and 7M Axle to firmly secure the battery box into place. A 5M Beam goes up in front on the top.

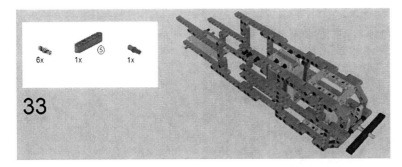

Figure 7-35. Add another 5M Beam with more Connector Pegs.

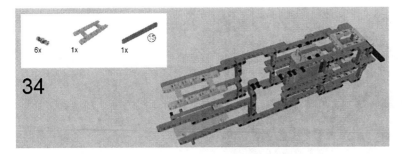

Figure 7-36. Add a 15M Beam and a 5 x 11 Beam Frame to the structure.

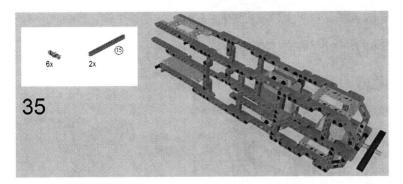

Figure 7-37. Add two 15M Beams as shown, as well as some more Connector Pegs.

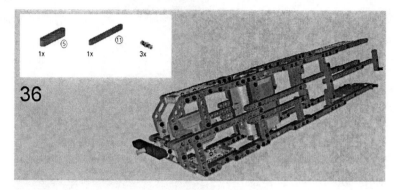

Figure 7-38. Insert an 11M Beam horizontally on this structure and then a 5M Beam vertically.

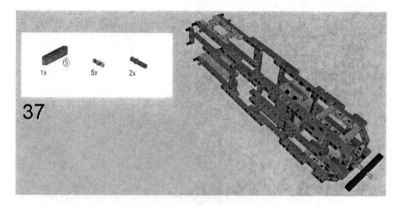

Figure 7-39. Add two 3M Connector Pegs and a 5M Beam vertically.

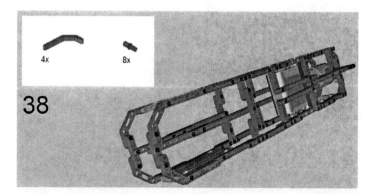

Figure 7-40. Add the last of the Double Angular Beams with Connector Peg/Cross Axles.

Of course, this is only the fuselage, and I am sure that you are anxious to give it wings. The next project offers instructions for a pair of wings, and I have added a way of building spinning propellers on these wings if you like. If you simply want the wings, just follow the directions without the propellers or motor and improvise appropriately.

Project 7-2: Creating a Multiple-Propeller Plane

If you are interested in Technic airplane models, you probably want to graduate from single-prop plane designs to building planes with two, four, or even more rotors. In this case, I recommend using only one LEGO Power Functions Motor and setting it up so one motor spins all the rotors simultaneously. If you want, you can use a motor for every engine, but you'll have to improvise on the instructions below.

Figures 7-41 through 7-66 deal with a wing-and-engine design that you can use on top of the fuselage that I detailed earlier. The way I have it set up allows it to fit on the top of the plane, but with some alterations, it can also go in the middle or bottom of the plane in case you want to follow that type of model.

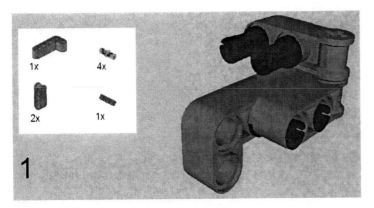

Figure 7-41. Connect a 3M Cross Block to a 4 x 2 Angular Beam. Put another 3M Cross Block on top; connect it with a 2M Axle.

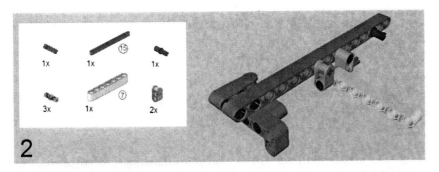

Figure 7-42. This shows the parts in Step 1 from a different view. Connect the 3M Cross Blocks with a 2M Axle, and then a 15M Beam. A Cross Block, Connector Peg, and Connector Peg/Cross Axle connect to a 7M Beam. Another Cross Block mounts next to the 7M Beam with a 2M Axle.

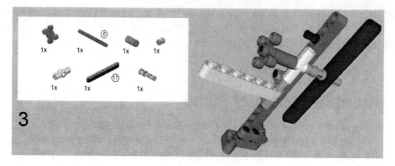

Figure 7-43. Create one of the first propellers by connecting the pieces together in the manner that you see here, and then join it to the 2M Axle.

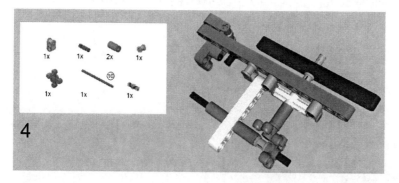

Figure 7-44. The 10M Axle joins with the Angular Gear and two Tubes with a Bush allow it to mesh together in a perpendicular method. The Cross Block joins with the 180 Degree Angle Element with a 2M Axle and Connector Peg.

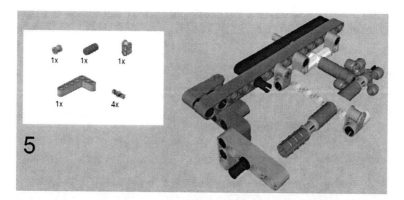

Figure 7-45. Add a Bush and Cross Axle Extension to the 10M Axle from the last step. Add a 5 x 3 Beam with Connector Pegs. A Cross Block joins here as well.

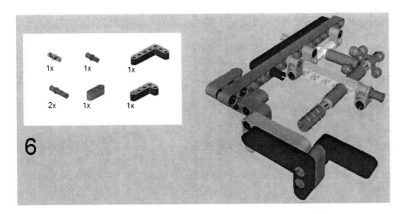

Figure 7-46. Add a 5 x 3 Beam to a 3M Beam and then a 4 x 2 Beam with 3M Connector Pegs. Connect a Connector Peg/Cross Axle to the Cross Axle.

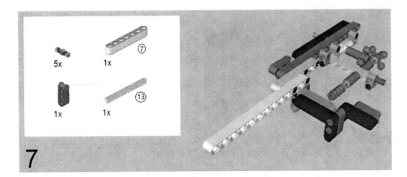

Figure 7-47. Attach a 7M Beam and a 13M Beam here, along with the 3M Cross Block.

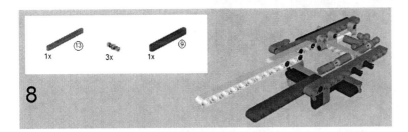

Figure 7-48. Add two more beams (9M and 13M) here along with the Connector Pegs.

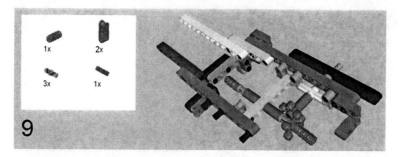

Figure 7-49. Note the addition of the Cross Block Extension to the Angular Gear. Join the 3M Cross Blocks together with a 2M Axle.

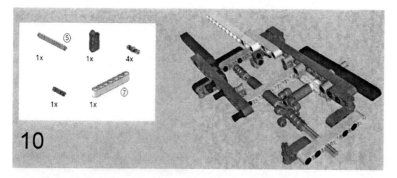

Figure 7-50. Add a 5M Axle on the Cross Axle Extension, then add a 7M Beam along with two 3M Cross Blocks joined with a 2M Axle. Note how it joins a 3M Cross Block from the last step.

Figure 7-51. Add a 15M Beam on one side with a 3M Cross Block on a 2M Axle.

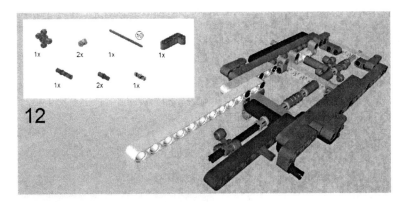

Figure 7-52. Add a 10M Axle along the center here, with a Bush and an Angular Gear. Add a 4 x 2 Angular Beam along the side.

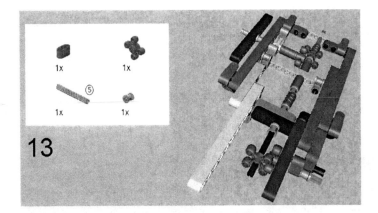

Figure 7-53. Join the 9M Beam with a 5M Axle, along with a 1 x 2 Cross and Hole plus an Angular Gear until it is meshed with the other.

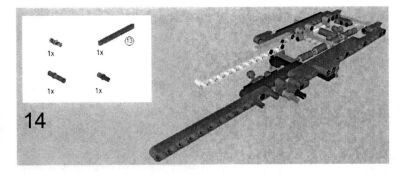

Figure 7-54. Add another long 13M Beam here via a Connector Peg, 3M Connector Peg, and a Connector Peg with Cross Axle.

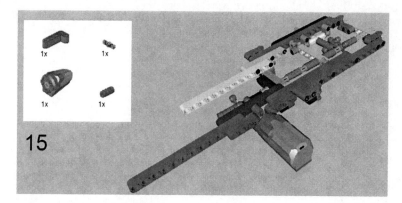

Figure 7-55. In this important step, join the M-Motor to provide the spinning power for the propellers. The 4 x 2 Angular Beam helps hold it on so the M-Motor spins the propellers but doesn't spin out of control.

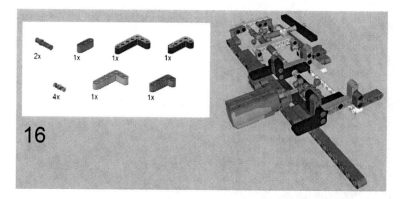

Figure 7-56. Two 5 x 3 Angular Beams, a 3M Beam, and a 4 x 2 Beam join together thanks to some Connector Pegs and 3M Connector Pegs This is not joined up until later steps, so line it up as shown.

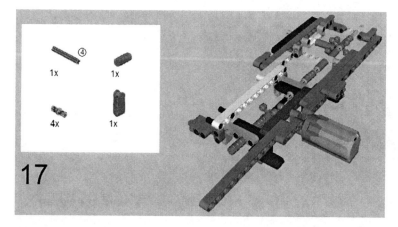

Figure 7-57. A 4M Axle joins the big piece made in the last step, along with another Cross Axle Extension.

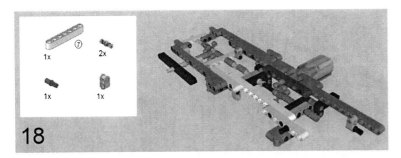

Figure 7-58. Attach a 7M Beam here, along with some other pieces like the Cross Block, Connector Peg, and Connector Peg/Cross Axle.

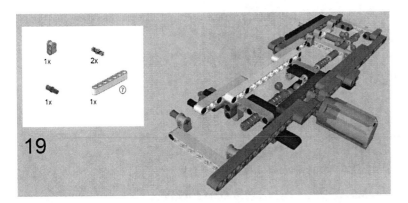

Figure 7-59. Add another 7M Beam here to mirror the one on the other side, plus a Cross Block, Connector Peg, and Connector Peg/Cross Axle.

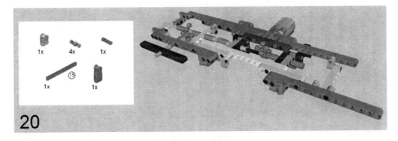

Figure 7-60. I switched the angle here so you can get a good idea of how to add another 15M Beam and other pieces like the 3M Cross Block and Cross Block.

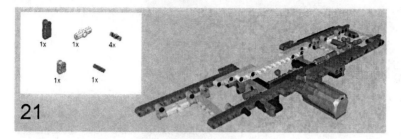

Figure 7-61. *You can see the 180 Degree Angle Element here attached as shown, along with a Cross Block, 3M Cross Block, and a 2M Axle.*

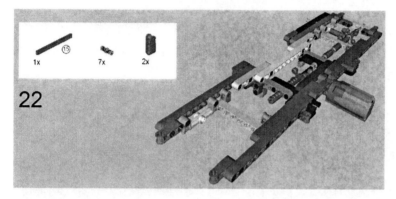

Figure 7-62. *Add a 15M Beam and two 3M Cross Blocks with seven Connector Pegs.*

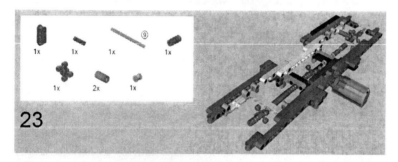

Figure 7-63. *A 9M Axle joins up with two Tubes, a Bush, an Angular Gear, and a Cross Axle Extension. This section joins with a Beam in the middle to power another propeller.*

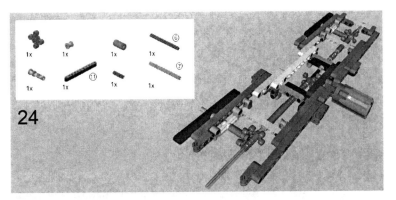

Figure 7-64. Join a 11M Beam with a Friction Snap, a 6M Axle, a Tube, and an Angular Gear to make another propeller. Note the placement of the 9M Axle, 2M Axle, and Bush.

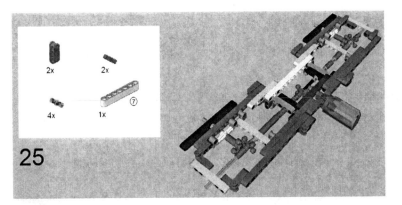

Figure 7-65. Attach two 3M Cross Blocks to a 7M Beam with four Connector Pegs. Use the 2M Axles to attach it.

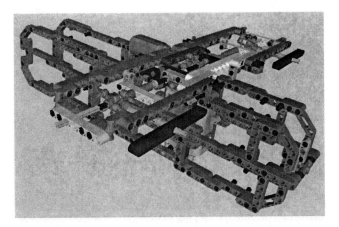

Figure 7-66. You can put the wings on the fuselage and start construction of a twin propeller engine plane.

You can change the motor from the M-Motor to the XL-Motor if you want, but you will have to find another way to mount it. Also, you can create similar wing sections to add on. Furthermore, you can add more propellers on either side by simply extending the axles that I deliberately left extending out 1M and creating propeller sections that mesh with more angular gear pieces.

You can even extend these wings and make eight propellers to model Howard Hughes' Hercules plane, the Spruce Goose, with Technic pieces. Yeah, I just challenged you. If you're up to it, watch *The Aviator* and create a wireframe!

Adding Power Functions and Other Features

The only thing that really needs power to be set in motion is the motor, and there is no point of hooking it up to an IR remote when a switch on the battery pack can do the same thing and still be in the same hand.

I found it rather futile to add in remote controls, as none of these LEGO Technic flying machines will fly. If they ever do fly, then yes, I will write a book on that. I look forward to the day when LEGO Technic makes pieces that will cause a vehicle to defy gravity, but I imagine that they will change the age limit on that.

But enough speculation. I suggest that you find out where you will be holding your airplane models and put a gear, lever, or some other type of controlling switch to make them do what you want them to do. Next I'll show you how to take control of your plane via landing gear, flaps, and even a rudder.

Project 7-3: Adding Retractable Landing Gear to Your Airplane

One of the coolest things that a plane can do is retract its landing gear, and there are ways of making this landing gear retractable on a LEGO Technic model. With the application of angular gear pieces, you can make all three landing gear go up with a twist. It is completely up to you if you want to make them motorized, but you will run into the problem of making certain that the speed is slow when they retract. I honestly don't recommend a motor. This project details a basic plan for something that has a spot at the cross axle that, when spun, will cause the three landing gear to retract or extend. See Figures 7-67 through 7-87.

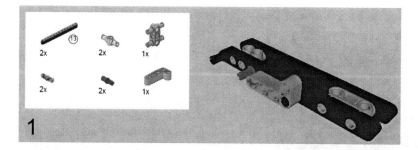

Figure 7-67. Connect 13M Beams together using a Double Bush and Beam with 4 Snaps. Use the Connector Peg and Connector Peg/Cross Axle as followed and use the same pieces to attach a 4 x 2 Angular Beam to the structure.

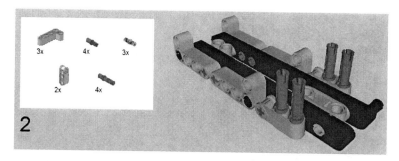

Figure 7-68. *Add three more 4 x 2 Angular Beams. Add a 3M Cross Block with a Connector Peg/Cross Axle, and then add four 3M Connector Pegs.*

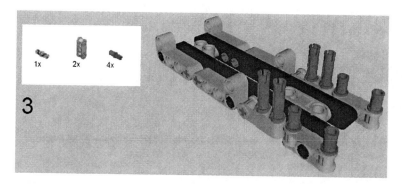

Figure 7-69. *Attach two Double Cross Blocks to the structure as shown, and connect two Connector Peg/Cross Axles on each.*

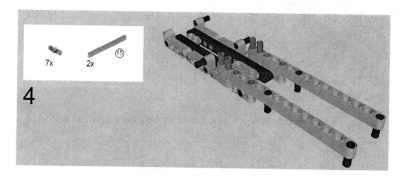

Figure 7-70. *Add three Connector Pegs to the 4 x 2 Angular Beams and attach two 15M Beams with the Connector Pegs as shown.*

Figure 7-71. Attach a 13M Beam to one side, and a 4 x 2 Angular Beam to that. Attach a Cross Block and 5M Beam to the 13M Beam.

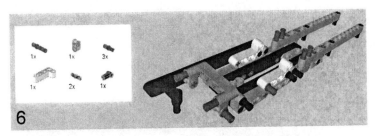

Figure 7-72. Attach a Cross Block to the 5M Beam as shown, and a Zero Degree Element to the 13M Beam. Don't forget to place the 4 x 2 with Connector Peg and Connector Peg/Cross Axle as shown.

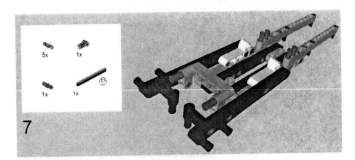

Figure 7-73. Add a 13M Beam so it looks like the other side, as well as a Zero Degree Element. Note the placement of the Connector Pegs.

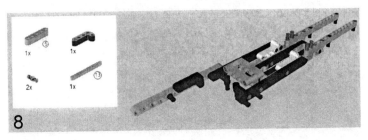

Figure 7-74. Attach a 13M Beam with a 4 x 2 Angular Beam with Connector Pegs. Don't forget to add the 5M Beam.

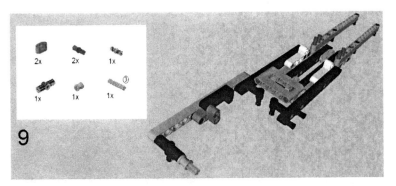

Figure 7-75. Add two Cross and Axle Beams in a perpendicular fashion as shown. Connect the 180 Degree Element, 3M Axle, and Bush.

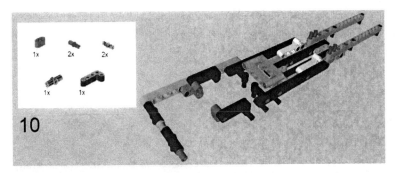

Figure 7-76. Add a 4 x 2 Angular Beam with a Cross and Hole Beam. Don't forget the 180 Degree Element, Connector Peg, and Connector Peg/Cross Axle.

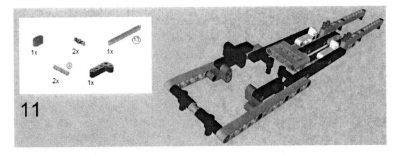

Figure 7-77. Add a 13M Beam, as well as a 4 x 2 Angular Beam on the other side. Use the 3M Axles to join the Cross and Hole Beams.

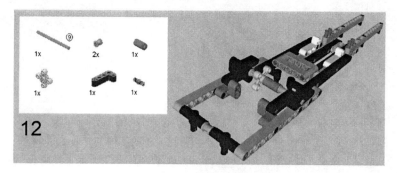

Figure 7-78. Use a 9M Axle to join two Bushes, Tube, and Angular Gear as shown. Don't forget to add the 4 x 2 Angular Beam.

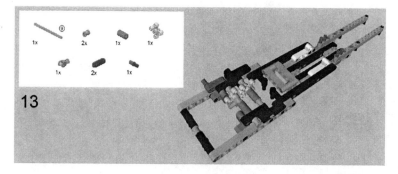

Figure 7-79. Use another 9M Axle to join the two Bushes, Angular Gear, Tube, and the Catch as shown. The two 3M Levers attach to a Connector Peg/Cross Axle.

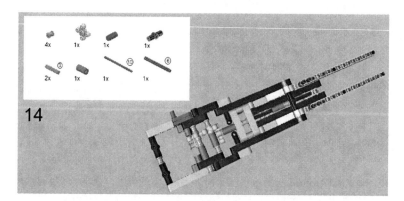

Figure 7-80. Focus to the central shaft with a 10M Axle, 6M Axle, Angular Gear, two Bushes, Cross Axle Extension, and Tube. Note how the 180 Degree Element connects with two 3M Axles and two Bushes.

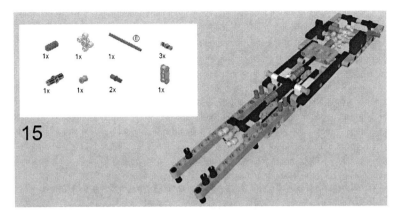

Figure 7-81. *Another Cross-Axle Extension joins with a 8M Axle, along with a Bush and Angular Gear. Attach the Connector Peg/Cross Axle with Double Cross Block, as well as three Connector Pegs.*

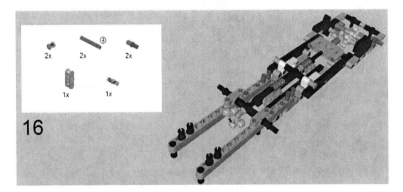

Figure 7-82. *Add another Double Cross Block and two Connector Peg/Cross Axles. Join the 180 Degree Element with two 4M Axles and two Bushes.*

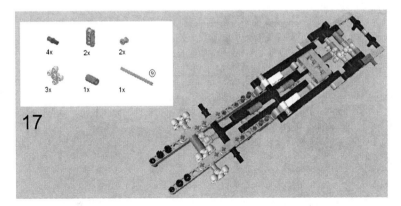

Figure 7-83. *Connect two Double Cross Blocks with the four Connector Peg/Cross Axles, and use the 9M Axle with the three Angular Gears, Tube, and two Bushes.*

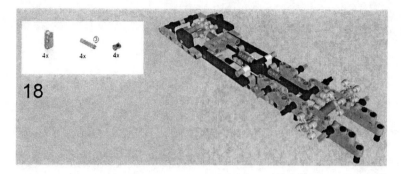

Figure 7-84. Use four 3M Cross Blocks attached to the 3M Axles and Bushes and connect them as shown.

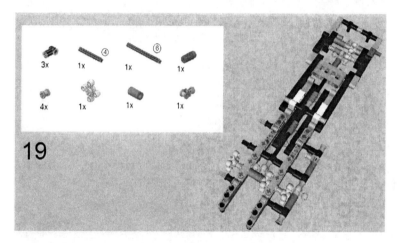

Figure 7-85. Use the three Zero Degree Elements, 4M Axle, 6M Axle, Cross-Axle Extension, four Bushes, Angular Gear, Tube, and Catch along the side as shown.

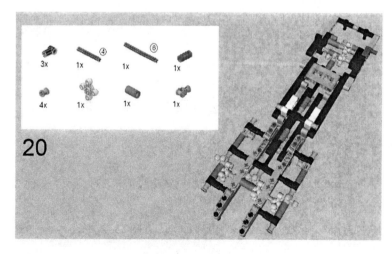

Figure 7-86. This step is a repeat of the last step, but on the opposite side.

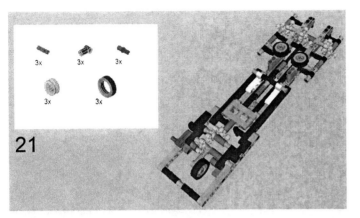

Figure 7-87. Attach a Zero Degree Element, 2M Axle, and Connector Peg/Cross Axle to the Catches. Add on the wheels, and the landing gear structure is complete.

Even though the fuselage of Project 7-1 was modeled after a plane that didn't have retractable landing gear, this particular set of retractable landing gear will fit on it. You can adjust it to fit your airplane model.

Now that you have an airplane, you will want to make it rise. In the next project, you will create some flaps for that purpose.

Project 7-4: Adding Elevators to Your Airplane

With the application of some axles and such, you will find that flaps are quite simple to make. I'm not certain whether you want to motorize them; I have found a simple non-motorized hand controller to work better.

You can use the following setup with the fuselage mode that I showed earlier. By turning the lever one way, the tail fins will rotate downward; turning it the other direction will rotate them upward. This makes the tail fin much more lifelike when compared to the elevators on a real plane. If you want to, you can design similar controls for the wings.

This project is just for the fuselage of Project 7-1, at the tail end. I only provide the parts that aren't in Project 7-1. See Figures 7-88 through 7-98.

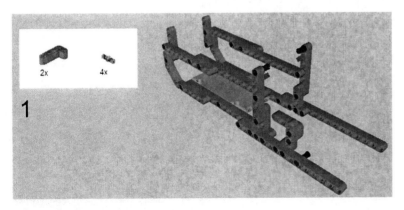

Figure 7-88. Start by connecting a 4 x 2 Angular Beam with another one with four Connector Pegs.

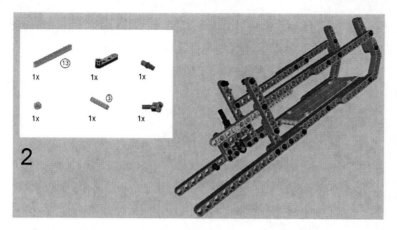

Figure 7-89. Add a 13M Beam with 3M Axle, 4M Lever with Notch, a Catch with Axle, and a Half-Bush as shown.

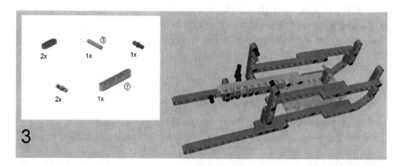

Figure 7-90. Attach a 7M Beam to the 13M Beam from the last step, and then a Connector Peg/Cross Axle with two 3M Levers and a 3M Axle.

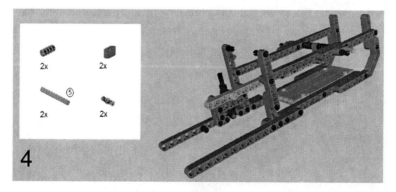

Figure 7-91. Connector two Cross-Axle Extensions on each side of the 3M Axle from the previous step, and then attach 5M Axles on each of those sides along with a Cross and Hole Beam and Connector Peg.

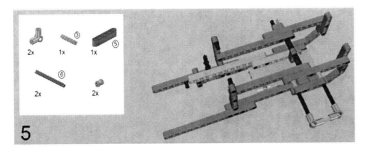

Figure 7-92. *Create a horizontal stabilizer by connecting two 90 Degree Elements, a 5M Beam, a 3M Axle, and two Bushes as shown.*

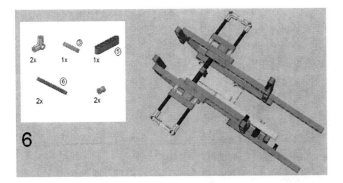

Figure 7-93. *Create another horizontal stabilzer as shown, using the same parts of the last step.*

Project 7-5: Adding a Tail Fin to Your Airplane

Now that you have added elevators to your plane, you should add on a tail fin, and you might as well put on a working rudder for that. See Figures 7-94 through 7-98.

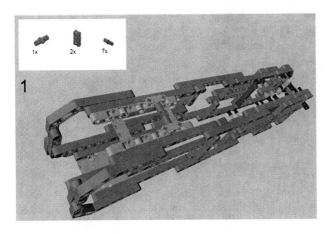

Figure 7-94. *Attach two Double Cross Blocks to the Connector Peg/Cross Axles, and then the 180 Degree Element.*

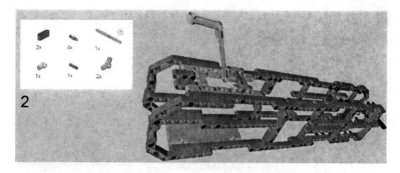

Figure 7-95. Add on two 112.5 Degree Elements with the 7M Axle, and the Zero Degree Element as well. Attach the 3M Beams with the four Connector Pegs.

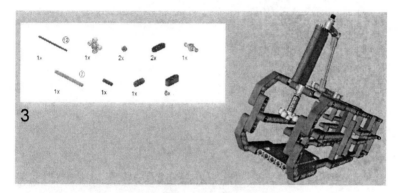

Figure 7-96. Connect the Double Bush onto the two 3M Beams. Slide a 12M Axle with two Half Bushes, a Cross-Axle Extension, an Angular Gear, and a 2M Axle. The six 3M Beams, the two 3M Levers, and the 7M Axle form the rudder.

Figure 7-97. A 6M Axle with Angular Gear, Tube, and Bush join here to mesh with the Angular Gear as shown.

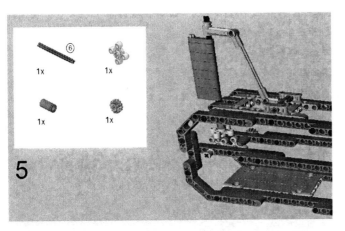

Figure 7-98. Add another 6M Axle with a Tube, Angular Gear, and Z12 Double Bevel Gear.

Project 7-6: Building a Helicopter

Building a helicopter is pretty simple, and this aircraft is the one that probably needs the LEGO Power Functions the most. After all, if a helicopter's top rotor isn't spinning, you don't have a helicopter—just dead weight. The trick is always to connect the upper rotor blade to the side rotor. This project is a simple set of building instructions for doing so; feel free to modify it any way you like. I found that the angular gears worked very well in this construction because they made a sound when spinning that was similar to that of a real helicopter.

This project is divided into three tasks: creating the main body, the cockpit, and the landing skids.

Creating the Main Body of the Helicopter

Steps 1-15 in Figures 7-99 through 7-122 detail the assembling of the helicopter's main body, which contains the battery pack.

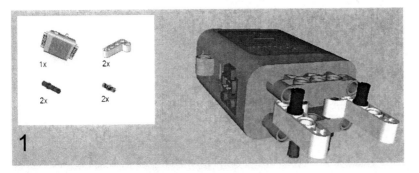

Figure 7-99. Start by connecting a battery pack along with two 4 x 2 Beams with 3M Connector Pegs and two other Connector Pegs.

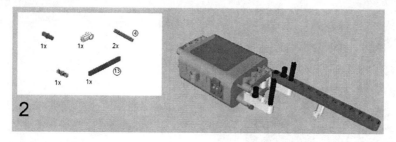

Figure 7-100. Add two 4M Axles. Then add a 13M Beam with a Zero Degree Angle Element, Connector Peg, and a 4M Axle.

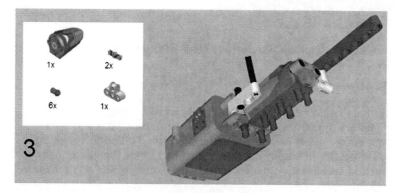

Figure 7-101. Attach six Conenctor Pegs with Knobs to the M-Motor as shown. Note the 3 x 2 Cross Block attached with two Connector Pegs in the front.

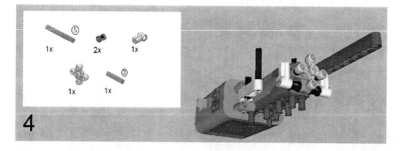

Figure 7-102. Use a 5M Axle, a Zero Degree Angle Element, and two Bushes to join the engine with the structure. Note the addition of the 3M Axle and Angular Gear.

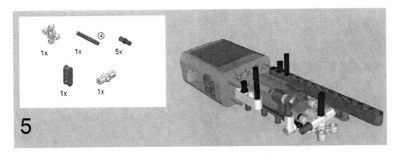

Figure 7-103. Add a 4M Axle with an Angular Gear to mesh together with the one from the engine. Note the Double Cross Block with the Connector Peg/Cross Axle.

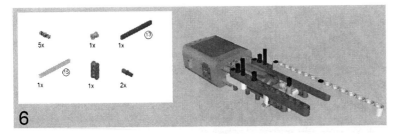

Figure 7-104. Add a 15M Beam and a 13M Beam on the other 15M Beam. Add the Double Cross Block and a Bush on the 4M Axle.

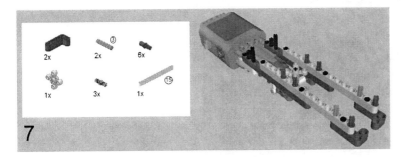

Figure 7-105. Add a 15M beam and two 4 x 2 Beams. Note the placement of the 3M Axles and the Angular Gear as well.

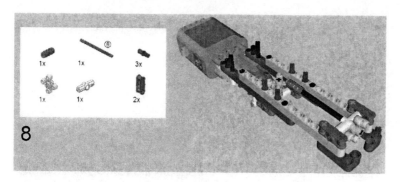

Figure 7-106. Add two Double Cross Blocks with a 180 Degree Angle Element, and then an Angular Gear and 8M Axle with a Cross Axle Extension.

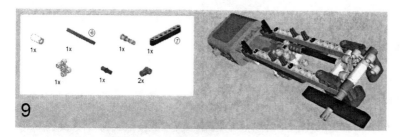

Figure 7-107. Add two Zero Degree Elements and a 6M Axle, along with a Tube, a Friction Snap, a 7M Beam, and an Angular Gear in order to form the side rotor.

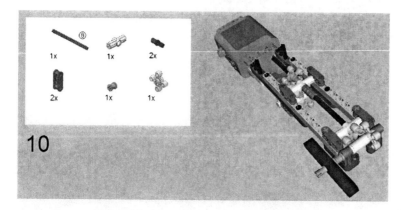

Figure 7-108. Add two Double Cross Blocks and a 180 Degree Angle Element to the 10M Axle with an Angular Gear, Bush, and an 8M Axle.

Figure 7-109. Add two 4 x 2 Beams to the structure. Even though you see an engine listed as one of the parts, all that is required here is to attach the other end of the connector. Also note the Cross Axle Extension.

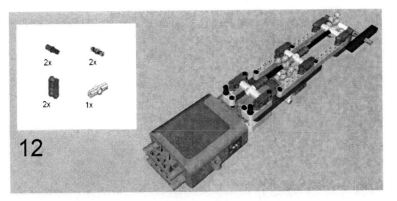

Figure 7-110. Add two Double Cross Blocks and a 180 Degree Angle Element.

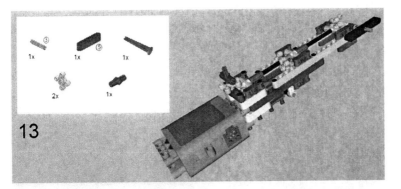

Figure 7-111. Add a 5M Beam; a 4M Axle with stop joins in the center of it with the Angular Gear. Note how this Angular Gear meshes with another by the 3M Axle, and note the application of the 180 Degree Angle Element.

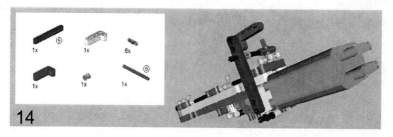

Figure 7-112. Add a 9M Beam to the two 4 x 2 Beams as shown, and then join it to the side of the copter with the help of the 6M Beam.

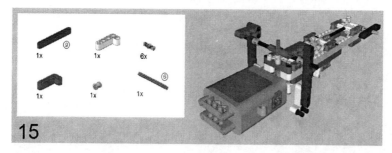

Figure 7-113. Like the last step, another side piece is constructed for the other side.

Creating the Cockpit of the Helicopter

In steps 16-24 (Figures 7-114 through 7-122), you'll create the helicopter's cockpit.

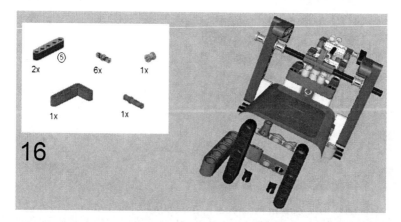

Figure 7-114. At this point, the emphasis goes to the front of the helicopter, as many Connector Pins are added, plus two 5M Beams. A 5 x 3 Beam is also added on one side. Don't forget to add the Bush on the 6M Axle.

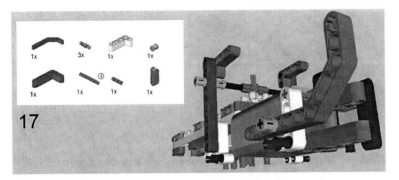

Figure 7-115. Add another 5 x 3 Beam. You can see how many pieces link together to form on the side.

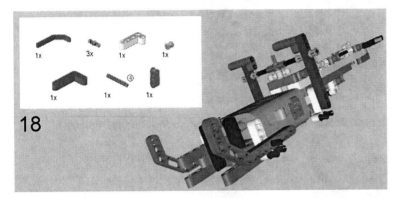

Figure 7-116. Gather the same pieces in the last step for the another section—a mirror of what you just made of the other side.

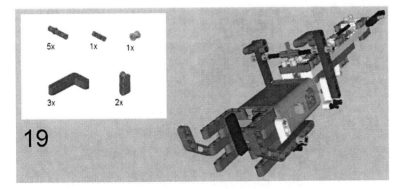

Figure 7-117. Add three 5 x 3 Beams plus a 2M Axle to make the side more stable. Add a lot of 3M Connector Beams as well.

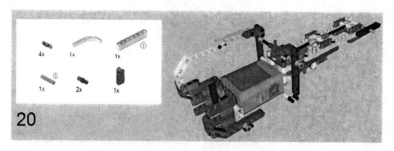

Figure 7-118. *It helps to have a Double Angular Beam as well as a 7M Beam to join together to form the side of the copter.*

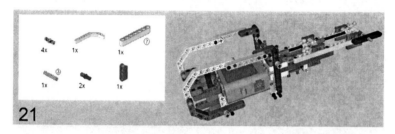

Figure 7-119. *Add more pieces so that the side is complete, which gives the copter a lot of symmetry.*

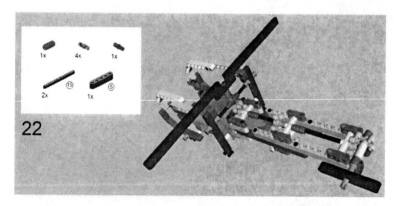

Figure 7-120. *You can see that two 15M Beams connect to a 5M Beam to form the top rotor.*

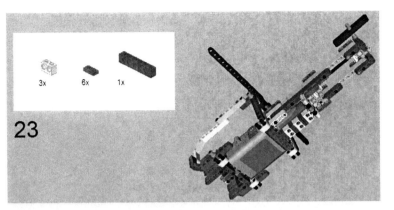

Figure 7-121. Add some traditional LEGO pieces in order to solidly connect the engine to the battery pack.

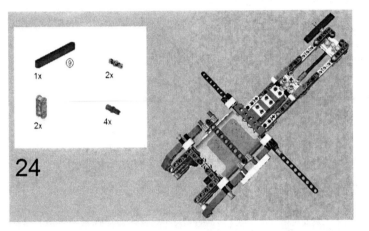

Figure 7-122. Connect a 9M Beam to two Double Cross Blocks and put this underneath the battery pack.

Creating the Landing Skid

In steps 25-27 (Figures 7-123 through 7-125), you'll put the finishing touches on the helicopter by adding the landing skid.

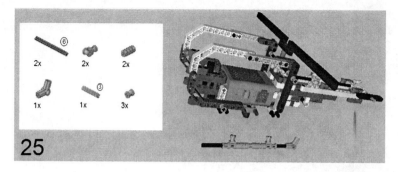

Figure 7-123. This is the first part of creating the landing skid, joined together as shown.

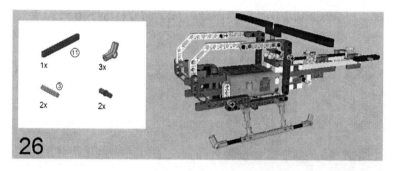

Figure 7-124. Construct the rest of the landing skid and add a 11M Beam.

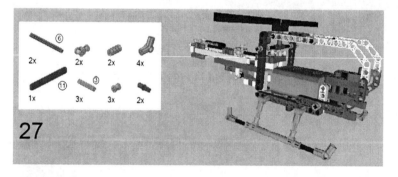

Figure 7-125. Repeat the last two steps so you have another landing skid, then add both landing skid parts to the copter itself.

Now that you have completed a helicopter, you can easily modify the frame until it is one of your liking. The important thing to note is how to hook up the motor so that you can have a rotating upper rotor as well as a spinning side rotor.

Summary

LEGO has always been in the airplane business, and if you want to make airplane models like the ones from Boeing or Lockheed-Martin, Technic pieces are the way to go. Not only can you use the studded or studless pieces to create an ample wireframe, but Technic pieces offer a chance to create an aircraft with some very cool features.

For example, a plane with a single propeller is easy to motorize as the motor and battery pack can be placed in the front. All you need to do is figure out what kind of propeller that you want. If you want a plane with multiple propeller engines, this is a little bit difficult: it requires a motor and battery pack plus a lot of gears to set more than one propeller into motion. This is very similar to the setup needed to create a helicopter.

In addition to motors, Technic offers a way to make your airplane feature-rich, like a real plane. There is a way to create a plane with landing gear that can retract and extend, as well as working flaps, elevators, and rudder.

In short, LEGO Technic has many ways to make your aviation dreams come to life. Granted, these creations may never actually fly, but this doesn't mean that you can make them as much like flying machines as possible!

Final Words about LEGO Technic

I hope that I have inspired you to figure out how to build LEGO Technic vehicles like cars and planes on your own. I have given you a formula for how to make a motor propel your vehicle, steer your vehicle, and give it some suspension. I've shown you how to create LEGO construction vehicles, airplanes, and helicopters.

I originally wanted to write this book to have fun with LEGO, and I have more than fulfilled this goal. I am pleased that there is an audience that is interested in this. In Chapter 2, I gave you some advice about LEGO Architecture, and I want to briefly review those rules here so that you remember them while you are building:

1. *If you build it, build it strong:* Remember to reinforce your LEGO model so that no one part of your creation is a stress point. Use axles and connector pegs to make certain it can withstand usage.

2. *Ease Your Pain:* Remember the basics of wireframing so you can create an idea for the frame of your creation and build around it.

3. *Go the Distance:* Always try to fit as many features as possible. If you can figure out a way to make a LEGO vehicle or other creation more realistic, do it. Plan for creating a propulsion motor and a steering system, as well as other realistic details like the lights.

I am going to add another piece of advice that will help you out as it helped me out writing this book: *Don't give up.* I'm sure you've heard that bit of advice before, but building with LEGO isn't about getting it right the first time. Sure, you can plan it all out in LEGO Digital Designer or the other programs that I detailed in Chapter 1, but you might find that your final product doesn't look at all like the digital design, even though you followed the instructions perfectly.

LEGO building is all about rebuilding. So my last bit of advice to you is this: *Build big and build original.* Create something that no one has seen before, or at least something that no one has seen before in LEGO Technic. Keep at it until you get it right.

■ ■ ■

Parts List

The following parts lists are generated by LDView. Part images are provided by Peeron. Circled numbers in the Part column represent part size in millimeters. Parts that come in more than one color are noted in the Description column accordingly.

Parts List for Project 2-1 (62 parts)

Part	Design ID	Quantity	Description
	2780	14	Technic Connector Peg with Friction and Slots
	32009	8	Technic Double Angle Beam 3 x 3.8 x 7 Lift Arm (red)
	32123	8	Technic Half Bush
⑮	32278	2	Technic Beam 15M (red)
⑤	32316	1	Technic Beam 5M (gray)
	32523	4	Technic Beam 3M (black)
	32526	4	Technic Angular Beam 5 x 3 Bent 90 (black)
⑥	3706	4	Technic Axle 6M

	3749	4	Technic Connector Peg/Cross Axle
	64178	1	Technic Beam Frame 5 x 11 with Open Center 5 x 3
	64179	3	Technic Beam Frame 5 x 7 with Open Center 5 x 3
	6558	9	Technic Connector Peg 3M with Friction and Slot

Parts List for Project 2-2 (47 parts)

Part	Design ID	Quantity	Description
	2780	12	Technic Connector Peg with Friction and Slots
	32019	2	Tire 62.4 x 20 S
	32020	2	Wheel Rim 18 x 37 with 6 Peg Holes and Long Axle Bush
	32073	1	Technic Axle 5M
	32123	2	Technic Half Bush
	32140	4	Technic Angular Beam 4 x 2 Liftarm Bent 90 (black)
	32140	4	Technic Angular Beam 4 x 2 Liftarm Bent 90 (red)
	32525	2	Technic Beam 11 (red)
	32526	2	Technic Angular Beam 5 x 3 Liftarm Bent 90 (black)

	3713	5	Technic Bush (gray)
	3749	4	Technic Connector Peg/Cross Axle
⑦	44294	2	Technic Axle 7M
	59443	1	Technic Cross Axle Extension Inline Smooth (dark gray)
	6558	4	Technic Connector Peg 3M with Friction and Slot

Parts List for Project 2-3 (61 parts)

Part	Design ID	Quantity	Description
	2780	12	Technic Connector Peg with Friction and Slots
	32019	2	Tire 62.4 x 20 S
	32020	2	Wheel Rim 18 x 37 with 6 Peg Holes and Long Axle Bush
	32062	3	Technic Axle 2M Notched
	32123	10	Technic Half Bush
	32140	6	Technic Angular Beam 4 x 2 Liftarm Bent 90 (red)
	32269	1	Technic Gear Z20 Tooth Double Bevel (gray)
	32270	1	Technic Gear Z12 Tooth Double Bevel (black)

	32270	1	Technic Gear Z12 Tooth Double Bevel (gray)
	32526	2	Technic Angular Beam 5 x 3 Bent 90 (black)
④	3705	2	Technic Axle 4M (black)
⑫	3708	1	Technic Axle 12M
	3713	4	Technic Bush (gray)
⑬	41239	2	Technic Beam 13M (red)
⑦	44294	1	Technic Axle 7M
③	4519	2	Technic Axle 3M
	58121	1	Electric Power Functions XL-Motor (Complete)
	59443	1	Technic Cross-Axle Extension Inline Smooth (dark gray)
	6538	2	Technic Cross-Axle Extension Offset (black)
	6558	4	Technic Connector Peg 3M with Friction and Slot
	75535	1	Technic Tube, Round (gray)

Parts List for Project 3-1 (89 parts)

Part	Design ID	Quantity	Description
	2444	4	Plate 2 x 2 with Hole
	2780	1	Technic Connector Peg with Friction and Slots
	2825	1	Technic 4M Lever with Notch (black)
	3020	1	Plate 2 x 4 (blue)
	32013	2	Technic Zero Degree Angle Element #1 (red)
	32019	2	Tire 62.4 x 20 S
	32020	2	Wheel Rim 18 x 37 with 6 Peg Holes and Long Axle Bush
	32062	2	Technic Axle 2M Notched
	32073	5	Technic Axle 5M
	32123	6	Technic Half Bush
	32140	2	Technic Angular Beam 4 x 2 Liftarm Bent 90 (gray)
	32184	1	Technic Double Cross Block 1 x 3 (Axle/Pin/Axle) (red)
	32184	4	Technic Double Cross Block 1 x 3 (Axle/Pin/Axle) (light gray)

32184	1	Technic Double Cross Block 1 x 3 (Axle/Pin/Axle) (dark gray)
32270	1	Technic Gear Z12 Tooth Double Bevel (black)
32523	5	Technic Beam 3M (white)
32524	1	Technic Beam 7M (black)
32524	2	Technic Beam 7M (red)
32524	2	Technic Beam 7M (light gray)
3705	2	Technic Axle 4M (black)
3706	2	Technic Axle 6M
3713	2	Technic Bush (black)
3713	7	Technic Bush (gray)
3749	10	Technic Connector Peg/Cross Axle
42003	2	Technic Cross Block 3M 1 x 3 (Axle/Pin/Pin) (black)
4519	6	Technic Axle 3M

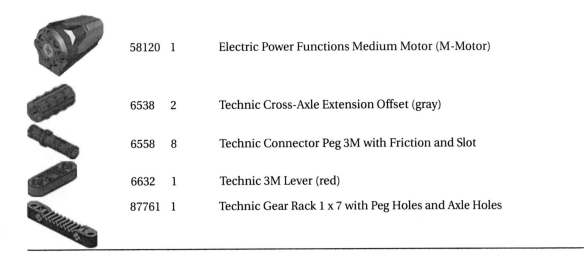

	58120	1	Electric Power Functions Medium Motor (M-Motor)
	6538	2	Technic Cross-Axle Extension Offset (gray)
	6558	8	Technic Connector Peg 3M with Friction and Slot
	6632	1	Technic 3M Lever (red)
	87761	1	Technic Gear Rack 1 x 7 with Peg Holes and Axle Holes

Parts List for Project 3-2 (35 parts)

Part	Design ID	Quantity	Description
	2445	1	Plate 2 x 12
	2780	8	Technic Connector Peg with Friction and Slots
	32019	2	Tyre 62.4 x 20 S
	32020	2	Wheel Rim 18 x 37 with 6 Peg Holes and Long Axle Bush
	32073	4	Technic Axle 5M
	32523	2	Technic Beam 3M (white)
	32526	4	Technic Angular Beam 5 x 3 Bent 90 (black)
	32526	4	Technic Angular Beam 5 x 3 Bent 90 (red)

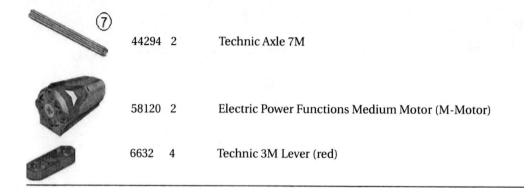

	44294	2	Technic Axle 7M
	58120	2	Electric Power Functions Medium Motor (M-Motor)
	6632	4	Technic 3M Lever (red)

Parts List for Project 5-1 (89 parts)

Part	Design ID	Quantity	Description
	2780	16	Technic Connector Peg with Friction and Slots
	32013	1	Technic Zero Degree Angle Element #1 (red)
	32019	2	Tire 62.4 x 20 S
	32020	2	Wheel Rim 18 x 37 with 6 Peg Holes and Long Axle Bush
	32034	1	Technic 180 Degree Angle Element #2 (black)
	32034	1	Technic 180 Degree Angle Element #2 (light gray)
	32073	2	Technic Axle 5M
	32123	4	Technic Half Bush
	32140	2	Technic Angular Beam 4 x 2 Liftarm Bent 90 (black)
	32140	4	Technic Angular Beam 4 x 2 Liftarm Bent 90 (white)

32269	1	Technic Gear Z20 Tooth Double Bevel (black)
32270	2	Technic Gear Z12 Tooth Double Bevel (gray)
32526	2	Technic Angular Beam 5 x 3 Liftarm Bent 90 (red)
3705	2	Technic Axle 4M (black)
3713	2	Technic Bush (black)
3713	4	Technic Bush (gray)
3749	13	Technic Connector Peg/Cross Axle
41239	2	Technic Beam 13M (gray)
42003	4	Technic Cross Block 3M 1 x 3 (Axle/Pin/Pin) (dark gray)
4255	2	Technic Shock Absorber 6.5L Cylinder
44294	1	Technic Axle 7M
4519	5	Technic Axle 3M
58121	1	Electric Power Functions XL-Motor (Complete)

	62520	2	Technic Universal Joint 3L End
	6536	2	Technic Cross Block 1 x 2 (Axle/Pin) 90 Degrees
	6538	3	Technic Cross-Axle Extension Offset (black)
	6558	2	Technic Connector Peg 3M with Friction and Slot
	6589	2	Technic Conical Wheel 12 Tooth Bevel

Parts List for Project 5-2 (99 parts)

Part	Design ID	Quantity	Description
	2444	7	Plate 2 x 2 with Hole
	2739b	2	Technic Track Rod 6M
	2780	8	Technic Connector Peg with Friction and Slots
	3022	1	Plate 2 x 2
	3023	1	Plate 1 x 2 (gray)
	32062	4	Technic Axle 2M Notched
⑤	32073	3	Technic Axle 5M
	32123	9	Technic Half Bush
	32140	2	Technic Angular Beam 4 x 2 Liftarm Bent 90 (red)

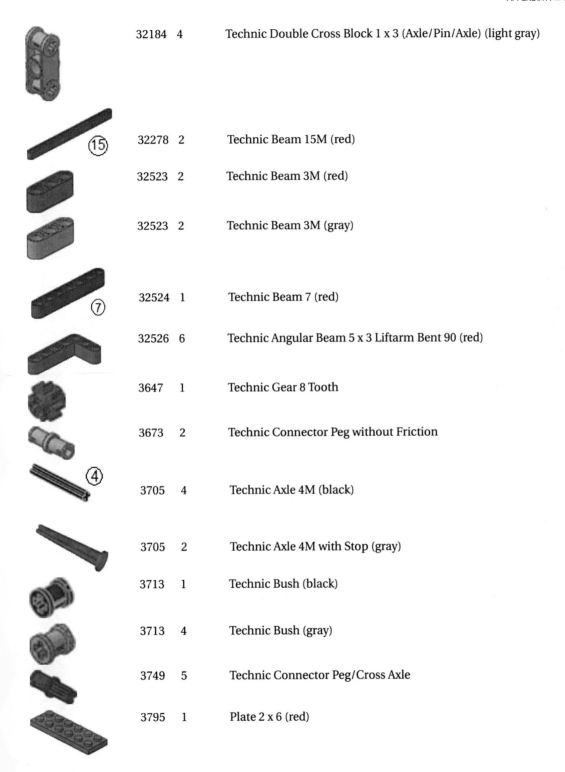

32184	4	Technic Double Cross Block 1 x 3 (Axle/Pin/Axle) (light gray)
32278	2	Technic Beam 15M (red)
32523	2	Technic Beam 3M (red)
32523	2	Technic Beam 3M (gray)
32524	1	Technic Beam 7 (red)
32526	6	Technic Angular Beam 5 x 3 Liftarm Bent 90 (red)
3647	1	Technic Gear 8 Tooth
3673	2	Technic Connector Peg without Friction
3705	4	Technic Axle 4M (black)
3705	2	Technic Axle 4M with Stop (gray)
3713	1	Technic Bush (black)
3713	4	Technic Bush (gray)
3749	5	Technic Connector Peg/Cross Axle
3795	1	Plate 2 x 6 (red)

	41677	2	Technic 2M Lever (white)
	4255	1	Shock Absorber 6.5L Cylinder
	4274	1	Connector Peg with Knob
③	4519	2	Technic Axle 3M
	58120	1	Electric Power Functions Medium Motor (M-Motor)
	60483	1	Technic Cross and Hole Beam 2M
	6558	6	Technic Connector Peg 3M with Friction and Slot
	6571	2	Technic Steering Arm 3H with Towball Sockets
	6572	4	Technic Steering Knuckle Arm with Ball
	6574	1	Technic Gear Rack with Balls
	6632	2	Technic 3M Lever (gray)
	6632	1	Technic 3M Lever (red)

Parts List for Project 5-3 (253 parts)

Part	Design ID	Quantity	Description
	2444	4	Plate 2 x 2 with Hole
	2780	42	Technic Connector Peg with Friction and Slots
	2825	2	Technic 4M Lever with Notch (yellow)
	3020	1	Plate 2 x 4 (red)
	32013	8	Technic Zero Degree Angle Element #1 (red)
	32013	4	Technic Zero Degree Angle Element #1 (white)
	32034	2	Technic 180 Degree Angle Element #2 (red)
	32054	2	Technic Friction Snap with Cross Axle (black)
	32062	9	Technic Axle 2M Notched
	32073	4	Technic Axle 5
	32123	16	Technic Half Bush
	32140	2	Technic Angular Beam 4 x 2 Liftarm Bent 90 (black)
	32184	1	Technic Double Cross Block 1 x 3 (Axle/Pin/Axle) (black)
	32184	7	Technic Double Cross Block 1 x 3 (Axle/Pin/Axle) (light gray)

32184	2	Technic Double Cross Block 1 x 3 (Axle/Pin/Axle) (dark gray)
32269	1	Technic Gear Z20 Tooth Double Bevel (tan)
32270	6	Technic Gear Z12 Tooth Double Bevel (black)
32270	1	Technic Gear Z12 Tooth Double Bevel (gray)
32278	2	Technic Beam 15M (red)
32291	4	Technic Cross Block 2 x 1 (Axle/Twin Pin)
32316	6	Technic Beam 5M (red)
32523	2	Technic Beam 3M (black)
32523	2	Technic Beam 3M (red)
32523	4	Technic Beam 3M (white)
32524	5	Technic Beam 7M (red)
32524	3	Technic Beam 7M (white)

⑦ 　 32524　2　　　Technic Beam 7M (light gray)

⑪ 　 32525　2　　　Technic Beam 11M (red)

32526　2　　　Technic Angular Beam 5 x 3 Bent 90 (red)

3673　4　　　Technic Connector Peg without Friction

④ 　 3705　11　　　Technic Axle 4M (black)

⑥ 　 3706　7　　　Technic Axle 6M

⑫ 　 3708　1　　　Technic Axle 12M

3713　6　　　Technic Bush (light gray)

3749　26　　　Technic Connector Peg/Cross Axle

42003　6　　　Technic Cross Block 3M 1 x 3 (Axle/Pin/Pin) (dark gray)

⑦ 　 44294　2　　　Technic Axle 7M

③ 　 4519　7　　　Technic Axle 3M

58120	1	Electric Power Functions Medium Motor (M-Motor)
58121	1	Electric Power Functions XL-Motor (Complete)
59443	4	Technic Cross Axle Extension Inline Smooth (dark gray)
60483	7	Technic Cross and Hole Beam 2M
61480	4	Tire 68.7 x 34 R
64178	1	Technic Beam Frame 5 x 11 with Open Center 5 x 3
6538	3	Technic Cross Axle Extension (dark gray)
6558	6	Technic Connector Peg 3M with Friction and Slot
6632	2	Technic 3M Lever (yellow)
6632	2	Technic 3M Lever (gray)
75535	1	Technic Tube 2M (gray)
87761	1	Technic Gear Rack 1 x 7 with Peg Holes and Axle Holes
9244	2	Technic Universal Joint (Complete Assembly Shortcut)

Parts List for Project 6-1 (76 parts)

Part	Design ID	Quantity	Description
	2780	14	Technic Connector Peg with Friction and Slots
	32034	1	Technic Zero Degree Angle Element #2 (red)
	32034	3	Technic Zero Degree Angle Element #2 (light gray)
	32072	2	Technic Angular Wheel (yellow)
⑤	32073	4	Technic Axle 5M
	32123	8	Technic Half Bush
	32140	6	Technic Angular Beam 4 x 2 Bent 90 (red)
	32184	2	Technic Double Cross Block 1 x 3 (Axle/Pin/Axle) (light gray)
⑪	32525	2	Technic Beam 11 (red)
	3647	1	Technic Gear 8 Tooth
	3648	1	Technic Gear 24 Tooth
	3713	6	Technic Bush (gray)
	3749	4	Technic Connector Peg/Cross Axle

	41677	4	Technic 2M Lever (black)
	4519	4	Technic Axle 3M
	50163	1	Technic Turntable Type 2 (Complete) Black/Dark Stone
	58121	1	Electric Power Functions XL-Motor (Complete)
	60483	2	Technic Cross and Hole Beam 2M
	6538	2	Technic Cross Axle Extension Offset (black)
	6587	4	Technic Axle 3M with Knob
	87083	4	Technic Axle 4M with Stop

Parts List for Project 6-2 (58 parts)

Part	Design ID	Quantity	Description
	2780	6	Technic Connector Peg with Friction and Slots
	3022	1	Plate 2 x 2
	3023	1	Plate 1 x 2 (black)
	32056	2	Technic 3 x 3 Lever Bent 90

	32073	6	Technic Axle 5M
	32123	6	Technic Half Bush
	32140	1	Technic Angular Beam 4 x 2 Liftarm Bent 90 (yellow)
	32184	1	Technic Double Cross Block 1 x 3 (Axle/Pin/Axle) (black)
	32271	2	Technic Angular Beam 3 x 7 Liftarm Bent 53.13
	32316	3	Technic Beam 5M (yellow)
	32524	3	Technic Beam 7M (yellow)
	32525	1	Technic Beam 11M (yellow)
	32526	2	Technic Angular Beam 5 x 3 Liftarm Bent 90 (yellow)
	32556	2	Technic Connector Peg 3M without Friction
	3673	1	Technic Connector Peg without Friction
	3705	1	Technic Axle 4M (black)
	3713	4	Technic Bush (black)

	3795	2	Plate 2 x 6 (black)
	41677	4	Technic 2M Lever (black)
	4282	1	Plate 2 x 16
	4519	1	Technic Axle 3M
	58120	2	Electric Power Functions Medium Motor (M-Motor)
	6558	2	Technic Connector Peg 3M with Friction and Slot
	6632	2	Technic 3M Lever (yellow)
	75535	1	Technic Tube 2M (gray)

Parts List for Project 6-3 (100 parts)

Part	Design ID	Quantity	Description
	2780	23	Technic Connector Peg with Friction and Slots
	2817	1	Plate 2 x 2 with Holes (light gray)
	32013	2	Technic Zero Degree Angle Element #1 (orange)
	32054	4	Technic Friction Stop with Bush without Friction
	32140	4	Technic Angular Beam 4 x 2 Bent 90 (orange)

32140	2	Technic Angular Beam 4 x 2 Bent 90 (gray)
32269	2	Technic Gear Z20 Tooth Double Bevel (tan)
32270	1	Technic Gear Z12 Tooth Double Bevel (black)
32270	2	Technic Gear Z12 Tooth Double Bevel (yellow)
32270	2	Technic Gear Z12 Tooth Double Bevel (gray)
32278	2	Technic Beam 15M (black)
32316	2	Technic Beam 5M (orange)
32523	2	Technic Beam 3M (black)
32524	2	Technic Beam 7M (orange)
32524	2	Technic Beam 7M (dark gray)
32526	1	Technic Angular Beam 5 x 3 Bent 90 (black)
32526	4	Technic Angular Beam 5 x 3 Bent 90 (orange)

④	3705	4	Technic Axle 4M (black)
④	3705	1	Technic Axle 4M (red)
⑥	3706	1	Technic Axle 6M
	3713	11	Technic Bush (gray)
	3749	7	Technic Connector Peg/Cross Axle
⑬	41239	2	Technic Beam 13 (orange)
⑦	44294	1	Technic Axle 7M
③	4519	3	Technic Axle 3M
	58120	1	Electric Power Functions Medium Motor (M-Motor)
⑨	60485	1	Technic Axle 9M
	64781	2	Technic Gear Rack 1 x 13 with Peg Holes and Axle Holes
	6536	1	Technic Cross Block 90 Degrees 1 x 2 (Axle/Pin)

	6538	2	Technic Cross Axle Extension Offset (black)
	6558	4	Technic Connector Peg 3M with Friction and Slot
	75535	1	Technic Tube 2M (gray)

Parts List for Project 6-4 (196 parts)

Part	Design ID	Quantity	Description
	2420	1	Plate 2 x 2 Corner
	2780	35	Technic Connector Peg with Friction and Slots
	3023	1	Plate 1 x 2 (black)
	3032	1	Plate 4 x 6
	32013	1	Technic Zero Degree Element #1 (red)
	32054	1	Technic Friction Snap (black)
	32054	2	Technic Friction Snap without Friction
	32062	1	Technic Axle 2M Notched
	32123	4	Technic Half Bush
	32140	8	Technic Angular Beam 4 x 2 Liftarm Bent 90 (black)
	32140	2	Technic Angular Beam 4 x 2 Liftarm Bent 90 (red)

32184	4	Technic Double Cross Block 1 x 3 (Axle/Pin/Axle) (light gray)
32269	1	Technic Gear Z20 Tooth Double Bevel (black)
32269	4	Technic Gear Z20 Tooth Double Bevel (tan)
32270	8	Technic Gear Z12 Tooth Double Bevel (gray)
32316	6	Technic Beam 5M (black)
32316	1	Technic Beam 5M (red)
32523	5	Technic Beam 3M (black)
32523	1	Technic Beam 3M (red)
32524	2	Technic Beam 7M (black)
32526	2	Technic Angular Beam 5 x 3 Bent 90 (black)
32526	7	Technic Angular Beam 5 x 3 Bent 90 (red)
3482	1	Wheel Hub 8 x 17.5 with Axle Hole

	3666	1	Plate 1 x 6
④	3705	5	Technic Axle 4M (black)
⑧	3707	4	Technic Axle 8M
	3710	1	Plate 1 x 4
	3713	22	Technic Bush (gray)
	3749	15	Technic Connector Peg/Cross Axle
⑬	41239	4	Technic Beam 13M (red)
⑬	41239	1	Technic Beam 13M (gray)
③	4519	2	Technic Axle 3M
	58120	2	Electric Power Functions Medium Motor (M-Motor)
	60483	3	Technic Cross and Hole Beam 2M
⑨	60485	6	Technic Axle 9M

	64781	1	Technic Gear Rack 1 x 13 with Peg Holes and Axle Holes
	6536	8	Technic Cross Block 90 Degrees1 x 2 (Axle/Pin)
	6558	14	Technic Connector Peg 3M with Friction and Slot
	6632	4	Technic 3M Lever (red)
	75535	2	Technic Tube 2M (black)
	75535	2	Technic Tube 2M (gray)

Parts List for Project 6-5 (76 parts)

Part	Design ID	Quantity	Description
	2780	15	Technic Connector Peg with Friction and Slots
	2817	3	Plate 2 x 2 with Holes (black)
	32034	2	Technic 180 Angle Degree Angle Element #2 (red)
	32034	1	Technic 180 Angle Degree Angle Element #2 (light gray)
	32123	4	Technic Half Bush
	32140	2	Technic Angular Beam 4 x 2 Liftarm Bent 90 (red)
	32140	2	Technic Angular Beam 4 x 2 Liftarm Bent 90 (white)

	32316	4	Technic Beam 5M (white)
	32523	2	Technic Beam 3M (black)
	32526	6	Technic Angular Beam 5 x 3 Bent 90 (red)
	3648	1	Technic Gear 24 Tooth
	3705	1	Technic Axle 4M (black)
	3706	1	Technic Axle 6M
	3707	1	Technic Axle 8M
	3713	9	Technic Bush (gray)
	3749	4	Technic Connector Peg/Cross Axle with Friction
	44294	2	Technic Axle 7M
	4519	4	Technic Axle 3M
	4716	1	Technic Worm Gear

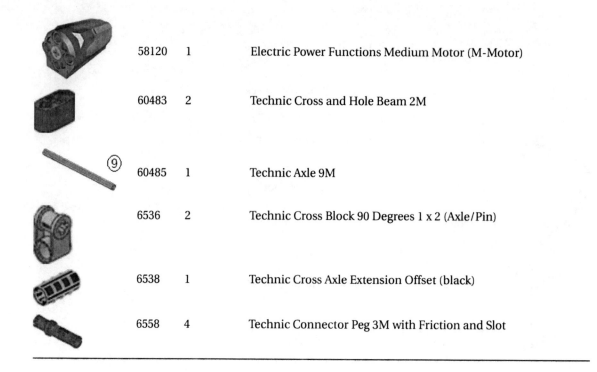

	Part ID	Quantity	Description
	58120	1	Electric Power Functions Medium Motor (M-Motor)
	60483	2	Technic Cross and Hole Beam 2M
	60485	1	Technic Axle 9M
	6536	2	Technic Cross Block 90 Degrees 1 x 2 (Axle/Pin)
	6538	1	Technic Cross Axle Extension Offset (black)
	6558	4	Technic Connector Peg 3M with Friction and Slot

Parts List for Project 7-1 (239 parts)

Part	Design ID	Quantity	Description
	2780	126	Technic Connector Peg with Friction and Slots
	32009	8	Technic Double Angular Beam 3 x 3.8 x 7 Liftarm Bent 45 (red)
	32034	1	Technic 180 Degree Angle Element #2 (dark gray)
	32054	1	Technic Friction Snap with Stop Bush (gray)
	32140	4	Technic Angular Beam 4 x 2 Liftarm Bent 90 (blue)
	32140	8	Technic Angular Beam 4 x 2 Liftarm Bent 90 (red)

⑮	32278	10	Technic Beam 15M (red)
⑤	32316	8	Technic Beam 5M (red)
⑤	32316	2	Technic Beam 5M (gray)
	32523	1	Technic Beam 3M (red)
⑦	32524	2	Technic Beam 7M (red)
⑪	32525	1	Technic Beam 11M (black)
⑪	32525	2	Technic Beam 11M (red)
	32526	8	Technic Angular Beam 5 x 3 Bent 90 (red)
④	3705	1	Technic Axle 4M (black)
	3713	10	Technic Bush (black)
	3749	26	Technic Connector Peg Cross Axle
⑨	40490	2	Technic Beam 9M

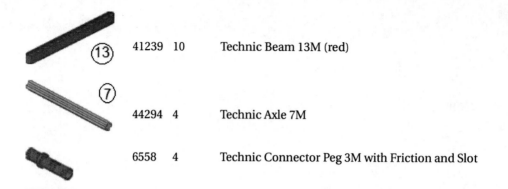

		41239	10	Technic Beam 13M (red)
		44294	4	Technic Axle 7M
		6558	4	Technic Connector Peg 3M with Friction and Slot

Parts List for Project 7-2 (183 parts)

Part	Design ID	Quantity	Description
	2780	66	Technic Connector Peg with Friction and Slots
	32034	2	Technic 180 Degree Angle Element #2 (white)
	32054	2	Technic Friction Snap (gray)
	32062	12	Technic Axle 2M Notched
	32072	6	Technic Angular Wheel (gray)
	32073	2	Technic Axle 5M
	32140	2	Technic Angular Beam 4 x 2 Liftarm Bent 90 (black)
	32140	4	Technic Angular Beam 4 x 2 Liftarm Bent 90 (red)
	32278	4	Technic Beam 15M (red)

	32523	2	Technic Beam 3M (red)
⑦	32524	6	Technic Beam 7M (light gray)
⑪	32525	2	Technic Beam 11M (black)
	32526	2	Technic Angular Beam 5 x 3 Bent 90 (black)
	32526	2	Technic Angular Beam 5 x 3 Bent 90 (gray)
④	3705	1	Technic Axle 4M (black)
⑥	3706	2	Technic Axle 6M
	3713	8	Technic Bush (gray)
⑩	3737	2	Technic Axle 10M
	3749	7	Technic Connector Peg/Cross Axle
⑨	40490	1	Technic Beam 9M
⑬	41239	2	Technic Beam 13M (red)

⑬	41239	1	Technic Beam 13M (white)
	42003	16	Technic Cross Block 3M 1 x 3 (Axle/Pin/Pin) (dark gray)
⑦	44294	1	Technic Axle 7M
	58120	1	Electric Power Functions Medium Motor (M-Motor)
	60483	1	Technic Cross and Hole Beam 2M
⑨	60485	1	Technic Axle 9M
	6536	8	Technic 90 Degrees Cross Block 1 x 2 (Axle/Pin)
	6538	5	Technic Cross Axle Extension (dark gray)
	6558	6	Technic Connector Peg 3M with Friction and Slot
	75535	6	Technic Tube 2M (gray)

Parts List for Project 7-3 (205 parts)

Part	Design ID	Quantity	Description
	2780	34	Technic Connector Pegs with Friction and Slots
	32013	8	Technic Zero Degree Angle Element #1 (black)
	32013	3	Technic Zero Degree Angle Element #1 (light gray)
	32034	4	Technic 180 Degree Angle Element #2 (black)
	32039	3	Technic Catch with Cross Hole
	32062	3	Technic Axle 2M Notched
	32072	9	Technic Angular Wheel (yellow)
	32140	4	Technic Angular Beam 4 x 2 Liftarm Bent 90 (black)
	32140	2	Technic Angular Beam 4 x 2 Liftarm Bent 90 (white)
	32140	4	Technic Angular Beam 4 x 2 Liftarm Bent 90 (gray)
	32184	6	Technic Double Cross Block 1 x 3 (Axle/Pin/Axle) (light gray)
⑮	32278	2	Technic Beam 15M (gray)
⑤	32316	2	Technic Beam 5M (gray)

	3482	3	Wheel Hub 8 x 17.5 with Axlehole
④	3705	4	Technic Axle 4M (black)
⑥	3706	1	Technic Axle 6M
⑧	3707	3	Technic Axle 8M
	3713	6	Technic Bush (black)
	3713	18	Technic Bush (gray)
⑩	3737	1	Technic Axle 10M
	3749	32	Technic Connector Peg/Cross Axle
⑬	41239	4	Technic Beam 13M (black)
⑬	41239	2	Technic Beam 13M (gray)
	42003	6	Technic Cross Block 3M 1 x 3 (Axle/Pin/Pin) (light gray)
③	4519	9	Technic Axle 3M

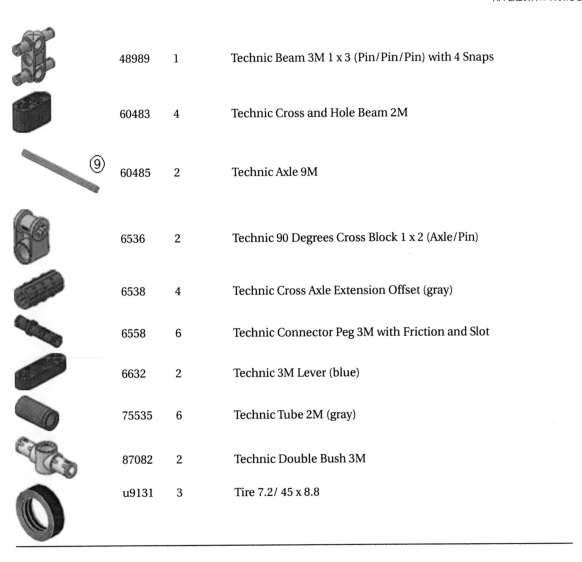

	48989	1	Technic Beam 3M 1 x 3 (Pin/Pin/Pin) with 4 Snaps
	60483	4	Technic Cross and Hole Beam 2M
	60485	2	Technic Axle 9M
	6536	2	Technic 90 Degrees Cross Block 1 x 2 (Axle/Pin)
	6538	4	Technic Cross Axle Extension Offset (gray)
	6558	6	Technic Connector Peg 3M with Friction and Slot
	6632	2	Technic 3M Lever (blue)
	75535	6	Technic Tube 2M (gray)
	87082	2	Technic Double Bush 3M
	u9131	3	Tire 7.2/ 45 x 8.8

Parts List for Project 7-4 (97 parts)

Part	Design ID	Quantity	Description
	2780	8	Technic Connector Peg with Friction and Slots
	2825	1	Technic 4M Lever with Notch (black)
	32014	4	Technic 90 Degree Angle Element #6

32073	2	Technic Axle 5M
32123	1	Technic Half Bush
32140	2	Technic Angular Beam 4 x 2 Liftarm Bent 90 (red)
32316	2	Technic Beam 5M (red)
32524	1	Technic Beam 7M (light gray)
3706	4	Technic Axle 6M
3713	4	Technic Bush (gray)
3749	2	Technic Connector Peg/Cross Axle
41239	1	Technic Beam 13M (gray)
4519	4	Technic Axle 3M
60483	2	Technic Cross and Hole Beam 2M
6538	2	Technic Cross Axle Extension Offset (black)
6553	1	Technic Catch
6632	2	Technic 3M Lever (red)

Parts List for Project 7-5 (285 parts)

Part	Design ID	Quantity	Description
	2780	4	Technic Connector Peg with Friction and Slots
	32013	1	Technic Zero Angle Element #1 (light gray)
	32015	2	Technic 112. 5 Degree Angle #5
	32034	1	Technic 180 Degree Angle Element #2 (red)
	32062	2	Technic Axle 2M Notched
	32072	3	Technic Angular Wheel (yellow)
	32123	2	Technic Half Bush
	32184	2	Technic Double Cross Block 1 x 3 (Axle/Pin/Axle)
	32270	1	Technic Gear Z12 Tooth Double Bevel (gray)
	32523	8	Technic Beam 3M
⑥	3706	2	Technic Axle 6M
⑫	3708	1	Technic Axle 12M
	3713	1	Technic Bush (gray)
	3749	7	Technic Connector Peg/Cross Axle

	Design ID	Quantity	Description
	44294	2	Technic Axle 7M
	6538	1	Technic Cross-Axle Extension Offset (gray)
	6632	2	Technic 3M Lever (red)
	75535	1	Technic Tube 2M (gray)

Parts List for Project 7-6 (258 parts)

Part	Design ID	Quantity	Description
	2780	54	Technic Connector Peg with Friction and Slots
	3023	6	Plate 1 x 2 (blue)
	32000	3	Technic Brick 1 x 2 with Holes
	32009	2	Technic Double Angular Beam 3 x 3.8 x 7 Liftarm Bent 45 Double (blue)
	32009	2	Technic Double Angular Beam 3 x 3.8 x 7 Liftarm Bent 45 Double (white)
	32039	4	Technic Catch
	32013	2	Technic Zero Degree Angle Element #1 (dark gray)
	32013	2	Technic Zero Degree Angle Element #1 (white)
	32015	4	Technic 112.5 Degree Angle Element #5
	32015	4	Technic 112.5 Degree Angle Element #5
	32034	1	Technic 180 Degree Angle Element #2 (blue)

32034	4	Technic 180 Degree Angle Element #2 (light gray)
32054	1	Technic Friction Snap with Stop Bush (gray)
32062	2	Technic Axle 2M Notched
32072	8	Technic Angular Wheel (yellow)
32073	1	Technic Axle 5M
32140	4	Technic Angular Beam 4 x 2 Liftarm Bent 90 (blue)
32140	8	Technic Angular Beam 4 x 2 Liftarm Bent 90 (white)
32184	2	Technic Double Cross Block 1 x 3 (Axle/Pin/Axle) (light gray)
32184	8	Technic Double Cross Block 1 x 3 (Axle/Pin/Axle) (dark gray)
32278	2	Technic Beam 15M (black)
32278	2	Technic Beam 15M (gray)
32316	3	Technic Beam 5M (black)
32316	1	Technic Beam 5M (blue)

	32524	1	Technic Beam 7M (black)
	32524	2	Technic Beam 7M (light gray)
	32525	2	Technic Beam 11M (blue)
	32526	6	Technic Angular Beam 5 x 3 Bent 90 (blue)
	3705	5	Technic Axle 4M (black)
	3706	7	Technic Axle 6M
	3707	2	Technic Axle 8M
	3713	2	Technic Bush (black)
	3713	14	Technic Bush (gray)
	3749	37	Technic Connector Peg/Cross-Axle
	3894	1	Technic Brick 1 x 6 with Holes

	40490	3	Technic Beam 9M
⑨			
	41239	2	Technic Beam 13M (blue)
⑬			
	42003	6	Technic Cross Block 3M 1 x 3 (Axle/Pin/Pin) (dark gray)
	4274	6	Technic Connector Peg with Knob
	4519	12	Technic Axle 3M
③			
	58119	1	Electric Power Functions 9V Battery Box (Complete)
	58120	1	Electric Power Functions Medium Motor (M-Motor)
	59443	4	Technic Cross-Axle Extension Inline Smooth (light gray)
	63869	1	Technic Cross Block 3 x 2
	6538	3	Technic Cross-Axle Extension Offset (gray)
	6558	8	Technic Connector Peg 3M with Friction and Slot
	75535	1	Technic Tube 2M (white)
	87083	1	Technic Axle 4M with Stop

Index

N, O

T, U, V

CPSIA information can be obtained at www.ICGtesting.com
Printed in the USA
LVOW120029271212

313374LV00008B/89/P